7 Steps to
LEAVING THE
RAT RACE

7 Steps to
LEAVING THE
RAT RACE

Free Yourself from the 9 to 5 Grind

A J A Y   A H U J A

howtobooks

I dedicate this book to my mother

Special thanks to Giles and Nikki, my family, Ellie and Asma

Published by How To Books Ltd
3 Newtec Place, Magdalen Road
Oxford OX4 1RE, United Kingdom
Tel: (01865) 793806 Fax: (01865) 248780
Email: info@howtobooks.co.uk
www.howtobooks.co.uk

First published 2004

British Library Cataloguing in Publication Data.
A catalogue record for this book is available from the British Library.

Produced for How To Books by Deer Park Productions, Tavistock
Typeset by PDQ Typesetting, Newcastle-under-Lyme, Staffs.
Cover design by Baseline Arts Ltd, Oxford
Printed and bound in Great Britain by Bell & Bain Ltd, Glasgow

NOTE: The material contained in this book is set out in good faith for general guidance and no liability can be accepted for loss or expense incurred as a result of relying in particular circumstances on statements made in the book. Laws and regulations are complex and liable to change, and readers should check the current position with the relevant authorities before making personal arrangements.

Contents

List of Illustrations

Figures

Tables

Introduction

I left my full-time job four years ago at the age of 27. At the time I had no strategy; all I knew was that I'd had enough at work. However, with hindsight I did have a strategy but it was not quite a conscious one. This strategy was simple but, for it to work, you need to have these three key attributes:

- courage
- motivation
- foresight.

Courage

I think leaving my job was the bravest thing I have ever done. Not only did I have a job but I had a *career*. A career with one of the most prestigious accountancy firms in the world, Deloitte & Touche. I was earning over £30,000 which at the time was not bad for a 27-year-old. My family were very proud of me working for this firm and amongst my peers I was considered a success. However, inside I felt like a failure. A failure to myself. I was clearly doing something I didn't want to do.

So you can guess their reaction when I said I was going to leave my safe, secure, well paid job – 'you must be mad!' Not mad but brave. Brave enough to do what most people are scared to do, brave enough to try to do things my way and brave enough to forgo life's little luxuries and to expect no less than 100% effort from myself.

It is likely that you will not get much support from the people around you if and when you decide to leave your job. It's not because they are malicious or anything. They will just be scared for you. This is why *you* need to be courageous. You will *never* be 100% sure that leaving your job is the right thing to do, and the people around you will further erode your confidence. If you are looking for certainties then leaving your job will always remain a dream.

Motivation

A successful business will not land in your lap! I've sat down and come up with over 100 business ideas, implemented about 10 of them and succeeded with only a few. It's no good just coming up with an idea. You have to believe in the idea and take it to the next level. You need to know whether the idea will work, and the only way of finding out is to implement it. This all requires effort.

I'm sure you've heard half-baked business ideas from people claiming they're guaranteed to work. Well, if they were guaranteed, why don't they do them? It's easy to say 'I don't have the time' or 'I don't have the money', but if it was such a good idea you'd find the time or get the finance. The reason they don't do anything about it is because they are lazy!

Now, I'm no 'Brain of Britain' but the beauty of business is that you don't have to be. It's all to do with the laws of probability. If you try enough times you will succeed. But to try takes effort. I've come up with some good ideas and some really stupid ones. I didn't know whether they were good or stupid until I had chatted with people and/or implemented them. With hindsight I would never have bothered with some of them.

Foresight

I'm not asking you to predict the future as this is impossible. What I'm asking you to do is to *think* about the future. You need to have some idea of where you want to be: having a mental picture of where you want to be tomorrow, next week, next month, next year, even the next millennium! Having this picture helps you to determine your actions.

When I left work my goal was to replace my salary with my self-employment work. I knew I wanted to earn £1,700 per month within three years. I wanted this income without having to do too much, so I chose property investment. I refined my strategy so I could earn my target income. Within a year I had achieved this. I was able to think about what I wanted, when I wanted it, how involved I wanted to be and what I was willing to do. I used my powers of foresight that we are all capable of using to help me determine what, when and how. Armed with these thoughts it was a lot easier to get what I wanted as I knew what I was aiming for!

My Previous Working Life

I met some great people at work whom I would never have met if I didn't work and I am grateful for that. I received some valuable training from my employer and I am grateful for that also. But apart from this I don't think I received much else. This was not my employers' fault – they were good employers – it was my attitude. I didn't want anything else. I wanted things outside work but I couldn't get to them because I was at work.

I'll let you inside my head for a typical day when I was at work:

8.30   [alarm clock goes off]: oh no, don't think I can get up. I think I'll grab another five minutes sleep.

8.35:   Shall I call in sick? I can't. I called in sick two weeks ago. My manager will be on my case if I do another sickie. My last excuse was pretty poor last time as well.

8.37:   I suppose I'll have to get up. Just another five minutes sleep though. I can get in five minutes late today. I was on time yesterday. They won't mind.

8.42:   Just another three minutes sleep. I'll get ready faster.

8.50:   Oh no, it's 8.50! Got to get up. Got to be in work for 9 o'clock. I'm going to be really late. Hope there's not too much traffic.

9.00   [get in car]: Damn. There is traffic! I'm going to be so late. I'll blame it on the traffic if anyone asks. I wish all the other cars on the road would disappear!

9.20   [arrive at office]: I hope my manager doesn't see me stroll in at this time. It's going to be so embarrassing walking in this late. I'll just walk in as if it wasn't my fault. Oh no, my manager is in! And he can see me walking in. Just say hello to him and then get to my desk.

11.00: It's only one and a half hours to go to lunch. Can't wait. I've got so many things to do in my lunch break. I just need to get all the things on my list done in my lunch hour. And I'm starving because I didn't have time for breakfast.

12.00: Only half an hour to go...

12.30: Hooray! Lunch is here and half of the working day is over. I'll have to get my skates on because I've got so much to do – and I've only got one hour to do it.

1.40: Oh no, late again. I'm glad my manager isn't here to see me come in late.

3.00: It's nearly time to go home. Two hours to go...

3.30: I'm so bored with work. Work is boring. I wish it was 5 o'clock.

4.30: It's nearly home time. I'll do my last burst of work and then get ready to go.

4.50: Come on 5 o'clock! I won't leave yet – I don't want to be the last to arrive and the first to go.

5.00: I can't go at 5. It's too obvious that I'm clock watching. I'll wait 10 minutes.

5.05: Oh sod it. I'm going to go now. At least I wasn't the first to leave.

5.07: Ah, relief, I'm free.

5.10: Damn. Traffic again! I wish everyone would get out of the way (again)!

5.40: I've got five hours now to do what I want. I think I'll have a drink with my pals.

7.30 [after dinner]: I've got three hours to enjoy myself because I've got to be up in the morning and I don't want to be late.

8.30   [arrive at pub]: Only two hours left of enjoyment. I wish
        I didn't have to go in to work tomorrow.
10.30: I don't want to go home. Some are going on to a club. I
        think I'm going to go. I'll just get less sleep. But I will get
        up because I can't afford to be late again!
12.30: It's really late. I'm so going to regret this in the morning.
01.30   [settle down to bed]: I am a silly boy. There was no need
        to go out and stay out so late! I hope I get up in the
        morning . . .

My life seemed to be regulated by time. I was controlled by it; I
was a slave to the clock. Everything I did was tainted by the fact
that I had to be in for work at 9.00 am and I could not do
anything else for the eight hours that followed – five days a week.
My Friday afternoons were heightened by Friday nights. My
Sunday afternoons were blighted by Monday mornings.

You might recognise some or all of these inner thoughts. Don't
be ashamed of them – people were not built to be regulated by
time. If you were, you would be a machine not a human being.
Being regulated by time so rigidly is contrary to how a mind
flourishes. Flashes of genius do not emerge according to some
timetable, they come out when the mind is free – free from the
chains of regularity and rigidity.

Through my work I meet a lot of employed people, all looking for
a way out of employment. They tell me about similar thoughts
and feelings and that they just can't take it any more. But it's no
good saying you want to quit but still want the lifestyle your
salary brings. You need to sacrifice, to change, to be inspired but
more importantly, to *work hard*. I hope this book will act as a

catalyst to creat these sacrifices, changes and inspirations but, for this whole formula to work requires a little bit of effort from you.

My Life Now

The lifestyle I have now is worth more to me than money can buy – even though it makes me more money than any employment could ever give me. I wake up when I want and I go to bed when I want and, in between, I do whatever I want. It's as simple as that. Everyday is a Saturday. Some days I will work and other days I don't. This is like setting aside the weekend to do some DIY work, to wash the car, fix the bike, etc., and you do it because you want to. You work to your own time and take breaks when you like.

Ironically, though, I work harder now than when I was employed. This is because I love my work, and the line between work and pleasure is very blurred. I find myself researching things out of my own interest because they are relevant to my work. Writing this book and sharing my knowledge is an interest of mine, so it just happens that writing books falls under the definition of work.

The following are some other lives. These are people I know; see if you can identify with any of them.

Brian

Brian has a well respected job with a venture capitalist company in London. He earns £45,000 a year and works a 50-hour week minimum. He has just met the girl of his dreams near where he lives, who he thinks he could marry but then gets told by his employer that he's got to go to South Africa for two years. They offer him US$70,000 tax free and living expenses, which he finds difficult to say no to. They offer to pay for frequent flights so he can come back and he accepts the deal.

Brian earns US$70,000 which equates to around £45,000 take-home pay, but he spends his weeks in a country he has no ties with, away from his friends and family and from the girl of his dreams. He spends all week working, some of the weekend travelling and the rest preparing for work and getting back to the airport – what a life! OK, he manages to save a significant chunk of what he earns, but is it really worth the sacrifice he is making?

If his intention is to save his salary and to invest it in a business then the answer is yes. If his intention is to use it as a deposit for a home then it is no. Let's say he does use it as a deposit for a home: then he has bought himself a liability – not an asset. People may tell you that a property is an asset but it's only an asset if it generates income, like rent. If Brian buys a home to live in he has to maintain mortgage payments for the next 25 years. This could mean he will have to remain a slave to corporate life and be at the mercy of his employer for at least 25 years. This is why people remain at work for longer than they wish – because liabilities are bought under the disguise of assets.

Arnie

Arnie works for a large, successful firm of solicitors. He's worked his way up to one below partner level and he's happy where he is. He's high up enough to choose his own cases but is not troubled with the overall performance of the firm as he's not a partner. However, the other partners are far from happy. They think Arnie should either move up or get the hell out! Arnie is then stuck between either taking on a position he doesn't want (although it is very highly paid) or leaving. Forced into this position, he agrees to become a partner.

Arnie now finds his workload and his responsibility increased but his social time decreased. He has been forced into something he doesn't want, even though his pay has risen significantly. It's a case of diminishing returns: he earned £95,000 quite comfortably but now earns £180,000 but has even less time for himself. Suddenly leisure time becomes a valued commodity, and a £85,000 pay-off doesn't compensate for his loss.

John

John, aged 32, is an investment banker who earns £50,000 a year. His boss and his boss's bosses earn significantly more, many of them over £200,000 a year. John knows that if he stays with the firm he will earn this too – it may be in three years' or ten years' time, but he is confident he will get it at some point. However, he realises he's not getting any younger. Many of his friends outside work are earning in excess of £200,000 already, running their own businesses. Five years ago John was considered a success and at the top of the pile. Now, compared with his friends, he is at the bottom of the pile. John now finds it difficult to get into his work and to stay motivated as he knows he could have done what his friends have done.

Mandy

Mandy used to work for a housing association. She found tenants, collected rent and evicted tenants if they didn't pay. She was very good at her job. In fact, she was so good that the rent she was able to collect compared with the maximum possible came to almost 99%! Void and bad debt expenses were therefore at an extremely low level.

Mandy made her employer but not herself very cash rich. But Mandy was not stupid. She set up a landlord income service focused on evicting tenants. It's her first year of business and she hopes to clear £10,000 profit – and all this in her spare time. She may be able to run her business full time in two years so that she earns what she's worth.

David

David is a self-employed property investor. His target is to earn £2,000 a month so he has to buy 20 properties to provide himself with £100 profit a month per property. While David acquires these properties with the full expectation of receiving £2,000 per month, he doesn't budget for tenants not paying him. So his £2,000 per month target soon turns into an irregular income of £3,000 loss one month or a £1,500 profit another. Living in London in a flat costing £800 per month and running a BMW, it doesn't take David long to realise that he's heading for bankruptcy.

What David hasn't done is control his fixed costs of living and be prudent (and realistic!) about his likely income. He must either reduce his costs of living (by ditching the flat and the BMW), control his credit better or expand and buy even more properties to lower the overall risk of non-payment of rent.

Anna

Anna told me she was so good at her job that she didn't even have to try! I asked her how good she would be if she really tried at something. She looked at me confused. I don't think it ever crossed her mind to give something her all. So I asked her what she would do as a vocation if money was no object. She said she'd love to run her own restaurant but didn't have any money to start it off. I asked her if she knew much about the restaurant business. She didn't. I asked if she had considered working in a restaurant. She said *no way*. She then protested that she was a professional, with a masters degree. So I asked her how these degrees had benefited her. She said a professional job that paid £33,000 p.a. that didn't even require much effort from her.

If Anna could step back and look at herself she would realise that she is doing a job she doesn't want to do, clinging on to her status and not doing a job she really wants to do. She has now left this job to travel around the world for six months. I hope she comes back with the intention of doing what she wants to do rather than what's expected of her.

Sonia

Sonia was employed by a major telecommunications company but was fed up with working in an environment where redundancy was a continual threat. So she took voluntary redundancy and decided to pursue her passion: life coaching. She got trained, had some business cards printed, created a website and got out there promoting her business. She used herself as the best marketing tool for her business, her rationale being that choosing a particular life coach will be based on whether that life coach's life is sorted or not. Because she was pursuing her passion it wasn't difficult to see that she was sorted! As a result, in one year, she amassed over 20 clients as well as several links with other businesses that provided further introductions. By the way, her website is *www.one2onelifecoaching.co.uk* if you're interested.

My auntie

If you want to know what it's like never to take a financial risk then look at my auntie. We all love our aunties I'm sure, but my auntie's lifestyle disappoints me considering she worked for 40 years. To her, the thought of losing even £1 of her hard-earned cash through an investment was too painful to consider. As a result she never made an investment and would be living on the basic state pension of £263 per month if it wasn't for her children. This fear of making an investment had not been thought out properly as she only thought of the downside, the potential to loses money. I am thankful that her pessimism didn't rub off on me. My uncle, on the other hand, is a heavy gambler, which means he takes extreme risks and I'm glad I didn't take on his optimism either!

Do you recognise any of these situations? Perhaps your situation is worse. Hopefully my lifestyle has whetted your appetite to free yourself from the rat race. So let's start with Step 1 – wake up!

Step 1
Wake Up!

Evaluating Where You Are Now and Where You'll End Up

Where are you now? Well, I suspect if you have bought this book you're probably employed, working hours that do not suit you and not earning enough. However, this might an oversimplification and not all of it may be true. What you need to do is to evaluate exactly where you are now. If you know where you are now then you'll have some idea of where you will be. Based on this evaluation, you can truly decide whether you like where you're at and where you're going.

Now, I'm not going to ask you whether you're good at working with people, are innovative, confident, self-motivated or anything else like that. These questions are impossible to answer as they are your own opinions about yourself and they're bound to be biased. But even more important is that the answers are *irrelevant*. If you do decide to go into business then these skills will come out without a doubt – you have no choice! When I started in business I was concerned that I was timid in negotiations. Four years on I'm far from it. If I now felt that I was being pushed into a deal that was no good I would clearly say so. I'm not going to sign a deal that threatens my business and thus threaten my lifestyle no matter how many people I would upset.

So how do we evaluate where we are now? Quite simply we look at the pros and cons of being employed. Let's start with the good news (if we can call it that!) – the pros of being employed.

The Pros of Being Employed

Regular fixed income

You receive a fixed salary at the end of the week or month regardless of the level of your input. There is little or no risk, the only real one is being made redundant or getting fired. With this regular income you can take on fixed costs of living which then determine your lifestyle – things such as houses, cars, clothes, going out and hobbies.

Food for thought
When you got your first pay cheque you probably had some idea what you were going to do with it. I imagine it was something similar to what other people do and have done with their pay cheques – spend it! It was your first chance to prove to the world that you were a normal working individual. You had a job and you could afford to do things other people who had a job did. This lifestyle soon takes over and becomes the reason why you work. It is then impossible to leave work as you become a slave to this lifestyle.

Is this regular income enough? While it's relatively risk free, is it what you are worth? Can this income ever rise to be what you are worth? Can you do all the things you want to with your current or projected salary?

How long will this regular income last? Perhaps your firm is in financial trouble and is looking to make redundancies...

Separation

Work life and out-of-work life, in theory, can be separate. When the working day ends your work commitments end and you can focus on your out-of-work life. You do not need to worry if trouble hits your employer as there will always be someone else to deal with it.

Food for thought

Should there be a distinction between your two lives? Wouldn't it be more sane to have one life rather than two? There is then no need for two personas. You can be assured of who you are all the time.

Does it serve any purpose separating these two lives, one of which is superior to the other? Just because it turns 5 pm, should you end your working day?

Separation isn't inevitable. If you have an over-bearing boss, a heavy workload or job insecurity, work life might taint your out-of-work life. Would it not be better if your working life and your social life were blurred? That is to say, working is socialising and socialising is working?

Enjoyment

Working for your current employer puts you in situations that you enjoy and that you otherwise wouldn't get to do, such as working with children, animals, etc.

Food for thought

You may enjoy your job but your ability to choose your hours is limited and the salary might not be enough. If you do enjoy your job this can be a great starting point for ideas for your new business. You may find that, even though you forgo certain situations, other equally enjoyable situations present themselves as you are entering an industry you enjoy.

Why not set up as a competitor to your employer? I know of several people who have done just that. They enjoyed the job they did, left their employer and set up as a direct competitor – and won!

Status

With your job comes a certain status in society which helps to contribute to your self-esteem, such as being a lawyer, doctor, etc.

Food for thought

You may enjoy the status the job brings but, again, your ability to choose your hours is limited and the salary might not be enough.

Personally I think status is all about self-importance. People work so hard to acquire status they come to rely on it to make themselves feel better about themselves and compared with others. Once you forget about what others think of you and you focus on yourself and what's right for you, the importance of status diminishes to nothing.

Social interaction

Your job exposes you to a wide variety of people or certain types of people whom you enjoy meeting and who form part of your social circle.

Food for thought

Nothing stops you from meeting these people out of work. You can always maintain your existing network of friends and build new networks. If you are a sociable person anyway then meeting new people shouldn't be a problem.

However, you may find that, through self-employment, you tend towards different people compared with when you were employed. Your attitudes will change and your existing network of friends might not change with you.

Education

You may benefit from training and education. Some employers spend a lot of money training individuals so that they are more informed and, hence, better at their job. These skills are transferable and help to boost your CV.

Food for thought

Some of the best training you'll ever receive is through experience. Experience is unconscious learning and is easier to digest. Through self-employment you will find yourself in situations that no textbook will have the answers for. These experiences will be more valuable than any training programme.

Now look at these pros! How many are applicable to you? Are any sufficient to keep you in employment? Before you answer, compare your pros with the cons of being employed.

The Cons Of Being Employed

Your time is not your own

You have to be in work at the hours dictated to you by your employer. If you are fortunate to be able to work flexi-time you still have to work a certain number of hours every week.

You are expected to get to your place of work at a certain time regardless of what you did last night or want to do in the day. You are expected to stay at this place of work for a set number of hours regardless. If you need to be home for whatever reason this is not your employer's problem – and nor should it be! Your employer pays you a wage so that you are there to take their orders during their specified work hours.

Food for thought

This is the single and most important reason why I left work and is, essentially, the title of this book. It's not about the money as money can only be spent; it's about time which, spent wisely, can be precious.

If you work a 40-hour week, take an hour to get ready for work and commute for one hour each way, work takes up 60 hours per week. This equates to over half your waking hours for one week! And, usually, at the end of the day you're too tired to do anything else. If you do overtime then this statistic gets even worse.

Were you put on this planet to live two days a week – Saturdays and Sundays? Or would you like to work when you want? Would you like to dictate your own hours rather than have someone else do it for you? Would you like to do things while other people are at work?

I never go shopping on a Saturday. I go in the week when the queues are small or non-existent, when you can find a parking space and when you can get there without getting stuck in a traffic jam.

The minimum retirement age is 60

In order to draw your pension you have to be aged 60 or over. So if you have no outside source of income other than your salary, your pension is all you've got to look forward to.

If you have financial commitments (which is likely) you will either need a salary or a pension. Hence you cannot afford to retire fully until you are 60 or over.

Food for thought

What a thought! I do not know whether I will reach the age of 60 and nor do you (unless you're over 60 now!). You may die having never known what it's truly like to not have to work to live.

Do you want to work till at least the age of 60? Do you have ideas or things you want to achieve before you're too old? Is the concept of working for the next 30 years too overwhelming? It's a big world out there and knowing you spend half your life in an office building, shop or factory may leave you feeling a bit hollow.

You may even have to work beyond 60 if your pension fund is not big enough to provide for you. The age of 60 is only a minimum!

Retirement income is unknown

Unless you have a very expensive defined-benefit pension policy because you are a company director (which is being phased out now) you will have no idea what your pension will be. It will fall within a wide range but will depend on the performance of the stock market and the annuity rates being offered at the time. Neither of these will be known at the time of your retirement.

Food for thought

How can you plan for retirement if you do not know how much you will have to spend? It can be very unnerving not knowing whether you will have enough, especially when pension companies perform so badly.

Owning a business opens up other opportunities of providing yourself with a defined retirement income, such as non-executive directorships, consultancies, licences and royalties, part-sale deals, complete liquidations and much more. If you do go into business you will find out about these opportunities in good time!

Effort does not always equal reward

Your salary is largely fixed. You may receive bonuses but these will be a fraction of your salary and may depend on the performance of others, which you have no control over. So it does not matter how much effort you put in; your reward – your salary – will never reflect your effort. Your reward will fit within a predefined scale set with maximums and minimums and will also rely on the performance of your peers.

Recognition for your work is also difficult to obtain. If you have an all-the-glory boss who loves to take all the credit or you are the only one in the team who has done well, your effort may not be recognised. More often than not it's the popular members of the team as opposed to the harder working members who get the credit.

Food for thought

Wouldn't it be nice to know that *all* your effort directly benefits you? Personally I think this is how people operate when it comes to work. You work hardest when you know you will get *all* the benefits from your effort.

Employees largely fall into one of two categories:

1. **Driven**.
   Employees who work beyond their strict duties because of the promise of promotion or more pay.

2. **Work shy**.
   Employees who do the least to keep their jobs as they are

demotivated. They are demotivated because they have no interest in the job or have no promotional prospects or want to do other things (like me!) or are simply too lazy to move.

Employees start off driven, become work shy and then move jobs. They then repeat this process for the duration of their working lives, never finding their true vocation. Do you find yourself changing jobs every two, three or five years? Do you find yourself jumping into a job you think will be interesting and then find that the same old feelings emerge?

You will never be rich!

If you look at this year's *Sunday Times Rich List 1,000*, you will not find one single employee. While the CEO or chairperson of a company is technically an employee, their wealth is derived from their *ownership* of the company rather than from their salary. The rich own businesses and the poor work for businesses – it's as simple as that.

I'm not just talking money here. You will never be rich with time which, for me, was my main motivation for becoming self-employed. An abundance of money has diminishing returns. Once you've bought your first Bentley the second and third have less importance. But time spent with your children is priceless.

Food for thought

There is no limit to what you can earn from being self-employed. However, there is a limit to what you can earn from being employed. It's quite disheartening to know that the only way you can become rich is by winning the lottery.

Even if you do earn or have the capacity to earn large sums of money, this will only last as long as you work there. You may only experience a high salary for a few years before you have to retire or the market changes. If you do well in business and set things up properly, the large sums can continue indefinitely – whether you do the work or not!

You cannot choose whom you work with

I think we've all come across this one! You may have a boss or colleague who is brilliant at what they do but you simply don't get on with them. It could be a personality clash, a cultural difference or opposite working styles. Whatever it is, you can't stand this person. The problem is there is nothing you can do about it.

This alone can cause a lot of stress. Having an overbearing boss who is always in your face, giving you impossible deadlines to meet and never appreciating your work can make you feel low.

Food for thought

Do you have feelings of hatred towards any of your colleagues? Having these intense feelings will only take from *you*. Wouldn't it be better to surround yourself with people you like *all* the time?

You can choose whom you work with or do business with if you are self-employed. There is no need for you to 'put on a face' for someone you don't like as you have no need to speak to that person. You will find that you will become a 'straight talker' as there will be no need to be otherwise.

When I started in business I had a few contacts who were a bit rude and condescending towards me. This was probably because I was younger than them and they thought they knew better. I simply refused to do business with them. Because money was not the motivation but freedom was, I was confident enough to say to myself that there is no need for these people to be in my life.

You will always be under someone else's control

Unless you're the CEO or chairperson there is always someone above you. So if they decide they want you to work out of your area then that is their choice, not yours. If they want you to change department that is their choice also – and so it should be as they pay your wages!

You may think you have control in your position as manager but the reality is different. Your promotion, pay, benefits and authority levels are all set from above which you have no say in.

Food for thought
If you are happy to take orders from someone else then you are merely a slave, happy to accept orders in exchange for a pittance.

I found the whole experience of being at work like being back at school. It seems very patronising for someone else to tell you when you should be working and checking all the time that you stick to his or her regime.

You will always have job insecurity

There is no such thing as a job for life. We live in a cut-throat business environment where employers will make redundancies if it makes economic sense.

Ironically, having a job is more risky than having a business as the employees are the first to go. If a business is facing financial trouble or it's more effective to out-source, they will get rid of you. If you own a business no one can get rid of you because it's yours! I'm not saying that you won't get in to financial trouble but, if you do, then the first to go will be your employees and not you.

Food for thought

You will have a better grasp of your security if you know everything about the business. The only way to know everything is to make sure you own the business.

If you remain focused in business then you can ensure that you will always be self-employed. Step 7 deals not only with how to build your position but also with how to *maintain* it so that you never go back to employment.

Prediction

So you know the pros, you know the cons – is it worth staying employed? I can guess where you'll be in the future if you carry on with this path of employment.

1. Comfortable

Comfortable – what an awful place to be! You will be seeing others achieve more and you will want more but will be too scared to lose your comfortableness so you stay there – never knowing what it's really like to be motivated by your own personal goals but motivated instead only by fear.

2. Underpaid

You will always think you are worth more. This feeling will never go away. Because you are paid for the hours you do rather than the deals you make, no amount of money can compensate for having to turn up for work when your employer says so.

3. Under-rewarded

The reward of money is usually not enough to make you feel good for the hours you put in. Recognition for your work *all the time* is also very important because it's *your* work. Recognition for all your work will mostly be lost within the system.

4. Overworked

As you get older your time becomes more precious. Responsibilities grow the longer you stay in a job, and so your employer will expect you to work even harder.

5. Insecure in your job

You will never be secure in your job as secure jobs do not exist. So this feeling will always remain.

6. Missing out

Because of the time demands your job brings, you will always miss out on certain things. As you have been working for a while you have simply got used to missing out on things.

7. Powerless

You will always feel you are unheard and that your opinion doesn't carry much weight. You're fed up with making recommendations that fall on deaf ears.

In summary, you'll be resentful, unhappy, stressed and tired.

Now, you may think this is a bit extreme. You may identify with only some of what I've said above, and that's OK. What I hope this chapter has done so far is to force *you* to think about where you really are now: I don't know where you are now because I don't know you! Are you heading in the direction you want to go or are you a little bit lost and wondering why you were put here on earth?

Take time out really to think if what you are doing is meeting all your needs now and will continue to do so in the future. If it does, stay where you are. If it doesn't, change! To help you change I'll tell you the pros and cons of being self-employed. I hope this list will whet your appetite and create the desire to change.

The Pros and Cons of Being Self-Employed

In a way the pros and cons of being self-employed are the reverse of the pros and cons of employment. But there are others. Let's look first at the summary of the reverses and then at the others.

Pros

The following are the pros and the reasons why they are pros:

- *Your time is your own.*
  No one is there to tell you when to work, apart from you. If you want to work late or get to work early, that is your choice. If you want to work from 9 pm to 5 am rather than from 9 am to 5 pm then do so! If you don't want to work that day, don't!

- *No minimum retirement age.*
  If you do well in business you can sell up or step down and let your business pay for your retirement. There is no law stopping you spending your profits for doing nothing – even if you are only 21!

- *Retirement income can be predicted.*
  Again, if you have done well you would have explored all the options available to you to ensure a guaranteed income from your business to keep you in retirement.

- *Effort does always equal reward.*
  If you do nothing you'll receive nothing. If you do something you'll receive something. But whatever you do you can be assured that you will receive 100% of the benefits flowing from your effort.

- *You can be rich!*
  There is no law to say that you cannot earn £1 trillion a year. There are no limits. The only thing that limits you is *you*!

- *You can choose whom you work with.*
  If it's your business you decide whom you deal with and whom you employ. You have 100% control over who enters your life.

■ *You will never be under someone else's control.*
Of course not – it's your business. Where you decide to surround yourself in whatever markets will be solely your choice. It's a highly responsible position to be in as this determines the success of the business.

■ *You will always have job security.*
Step 7 deals with this in more detail.

Cons

The following are the cons but why they are, in fact, *not* cons:

■ *Irregular income.*
It's true that your income will be irregular. Hopefully, you will have adopted Step 2 and will have prepared for this. This will mean that you will minimise your fixed costs of living so that you can weather the bad times. Once you are through these times then having an irregular income of £10,000 one month and £30,000 the next won't be such a problem!

■ *No separation.*
Who needs separation? Why not have a life that is not split between work life and social life? If you're interested in something, turn it in to a business!

■ *No enjoyment.*
If you will miss the enjoyment you got from your job, look for a business that is similar or that is in the supply chain of this environment. If you can't manage that then look for something you think you will enjoy. To ensure success you must have an interest in the product/service you are selling – I don't have to tell you this!

■ *Loss of status.*
Status means absolutely nothing! Okay, it might get you a table in a restaurant but is it really worth working over 40 hours a week for this privilege?

■ *Lack of social contact.*
If your time is yours it's up to you to maintain social contact. At least you can socialise with the people you want to socialise with.

■ *No formal education.*
The best education is experience. I have had the best training in life from college, university and my accountancy firm but it doesn't compare to the real-life experiences I have had in setting up my own business.

These are the reverses but here are the others I have found through experience. The following is not a complete list as I have only been self-employed for four years. I am sure there are more.

Cons

The following are the cons but, again, with the reasons why they are in fact *not* cons:

■ *Administration.*
People think there is a lot of red tape in running a business – and they're right! But the admin grows with the business. The more trade you do the more paperwork. However, it's a small price to pay for the increased business. If your business does well you can hire someone to do the admin. You do have to do everything when you start a business but if your business grows you can pay someone to do all the things you don't want to!

■ *Tax.*

People become so focused on how to avoid tax rather than focusing on how to make a profit. Remember, only profits are taxed, so first make a profit and then worry about tax. However, self-employed people are subject to the same income tax rules as employed people. Okay, this is done for you by your employer if you are employed but the amount paid is the same for those who are employed as for the self-employed.

■ *Responsibility.*

You do have to be responsible, but do you have a problem with this? Being responsible is part of being an adult so get used to it and grow up! However, it's easy to delegate responsibility when you are employed – 'it's the employer's problem'. There is, on the other hand, a lot of personal reward to be had knowing that the buck stops with you. When things go right you know you deserve full credit. When things go wrong you learn very important lessons that no course or training programme could ever teach you.

■ *Jealousy.*

If you do start your own business and have a degree of success some people will be jealous – it's only natural. You simply have to be thick skinned. Being self-employed teaches you a lot about how to ignore negativity and just to get on with things. Don't repeat the mantra – 'well, if they're jealous then they weren't friends in the first place'. Becoming self-employed is not just hard for you but for others around you as well.

■ *Apathy.*

It's completely normal that, when you become your own boss,

you will have bouts of apathy. I went through it. But if you are determined to make your business work you will ensure that they are only bouts and do not last for long periods of time. However, it is your right to do nothing if you do not want to. But if you have set goals in your business plan you will not allow yourself to do this. Apathy comes when you don't have to do things – and this is one of the perks of being self-employed!

Pros

The following is just one further pro, with a few points to consider:

■ *Prefer to invest rather than spend.*
When you enter the business world you understand that every £1 you have could either buy you something you want now or buy you something you want that's even better at a later date if you invest it. Knowing this means you intrinsically spend more carefully, investing the rest, so that you can acquire things you never thought possible.

Points to consider:
■ Do the things you buy make you feel better about yourself?
■ Would it not be better knowing that your time is more important than any material good?
■ Is it not better to invest in businesses knowing that you will have more time for yourself, your family and friends?

Now I know I have made a serious attack on being employed and you may think this is too harsh. If I had been reading this while I was employed I would have immediately defended myself and said 'I enjoy my job, I get to meet people, I get well paid, I have status. . .' because this would be normal. But try to see what I'm saying as an attack. Think through what you are doing and where you're going to end up! What your employer is offering you does not compensate for what you will have to forgo. It is only the work ethic that keeps you in employment because you know of nothing else.

Now I may have really rubbished what you and others are currently doing but it gets even worse. Step 2 is 'Living like a pauper'. To succeed you have to prepare yourself for self-employment and this means going without. Not for long but long enough for you to get established in business.

Step 2
Living Like
a Pauper

Minimising Your Fixed Costs and Raising Your Starting Capital

Living like a pauper will prepare you for self-employment. Why? Because you have to do the following three things to become self-employed:

1. Minimise your fixed costs of living prior to leaving your job.

2. Raise your initial investment to start your own business.

3. Maintain your fixed costs of living after leaving your job.

To achieve all these three things requires you to live like a pauper.

Minimising Your Fixed Costs of Living

The most important factor in business is cash. The fewer cash drains you have, the more likely you are to succeed. The biggest cash drain is the cost of living. If we can control that and keep it to the bare minimum, the easier it is to survive the initial stages of self-employment.

There are only two ways of minimising your fixed costs of living:

1. going without (i.e. not spending) and

2. cutting costs (i.e. spending less).

Not Spending

I'm not going to bore you about how you should stop smoking, drinking, eating or simply just indulging. What you should do is, when you get paid, put a certain amount aside so you can't get at it. Put it in a separate deposit account, give it to a family member or put it under your mattress – what ever you do, don't spend it! What will happen is that you'll adjust to the new level of spending you have at your disposal.

Always ask yourself – do I really *need* this item or do I just *want* it? If it's a luxury then it's probably a want. When I was setting up my business I went without. Here are some of the things I used to buy when I was at work but went without when I was starting self-employment:

- Newspapers and magazines.
- The use of a whole flat as opposed to shared accommodation.
- CDs.
- Designer clothes.
- Meals at restaurants.
- Nights out in London visiting trendy bars and nightclubs.

It was easy for me to go without. In the back of my mind I knew that if I went without now I would have in the future. This is now the case and I have a lifestyle most would envy. I hope this inspires you. Remember, saving for a way out can be very rewarding. When you have saved enough and started your own business, the results are very immediate – the labours of your scrimping and saving will result in you having enough time for your family, friends and yourself.

Spending Less

There are really only five things you can spend your money on:

1. Food and consumables.

2. Shelter.

3. Travel.

4. Entertainment and clothing.

5. Loans and savings plans.

Here are some tips on how to cut back in spending on each of these categories.

Food and consumables

Eating in rather than out
It's so easy to go to down to your nearest burger chain, Indian restaurant or Chinese take-away. There's no washing up, it tastes lovely and there is no preparation time.

However, you do pay for this. I used to make myself sandwiches in the poor days. Two slices of bread, a bit of lettuce and a chicken slice – total cost: 20p! Compare this with an Indian take-away costing at least £7. I'm not saying don't treat yourself. I treated myself to one chicken biryani from my local Indian once a week – but that was it.

Invariably the food you prepare at home will be healthier too. The irony is that, even though I can afford to eat out every night, I now choose to eat in as it is healthier. I even look forward to those chicken sandwiches!

Going round to your mum's!

This may not be possible for everyone. It depends, of course, on whether she is still alive, whether you still see her or if you live close to her. The principle is – don't be ashamed to ask for help. My mum quite enjoyed seeing me twice a week (or sometimes more!) and, likewise, there's no cooking like your mum's.

Do you have a brother, sister, nan, cousin or good friend who loves to see you? If you let them know what you are doing – starting your own business – you will be surprised how willing they are to help.

Do not think you are a sponger! *Always* remember the people who helped you to get to the top. As a thanks, my mum now receives an income from me that is in excess of her pension, and she doesn't have do a thing!

Non-branded goods

If you understand how supermarkets work, try this. A lot of 'own brand' goods are produced by the branded-goods manufacturers, so sometimes the quality is the same. Now I say *sometimes*! I have tried some of the non-branded goods and they taste awful, but there are some own-branded goods that taste as good if not better than the branded goods. So give it a try. The cost savings can be up to 50%.

'Buy one, get one free'

Every supermarket does this. They sell goods at no profit or even at a loss to get you through the door. You can use this to your advantage. If you have the time, you can go to every major supermarket and capitalise on all their deals. I have to admit, I never had the time to justify the cost savings. But if you have a family and you are willing to stock up, I would estimate that you can reduce your shopping bill by 40%.

Shelter

Renting a room rather than a flat or house

Having your own living space is a costly thing. It can sometimes drain your monthly income by up to 70% when you take into account the rent, rates, bills and insurance. Why not consider lodging? I did. It cost me £55 per week and I was able to preserve the cash I had saved. I lodged with someone for 12 months, who is now a good friend, so I could put a deposit down on my first house.

Do you really need all that space? Would your social life receive a boost from sharing with others? If you can do this it will have the most dramatic impact on your level of savings of all the cost savings mentioned here.

Switching utility suppliers

It's a competitive market out there when it comes to supplying gas, electricity and the telephone. Because of deregulation you can save up to 40% on your bills simply by switching, and it's easy to do.

Look out for new tariffs for your mobile phone. Prices have only come down and so there will always be a new tariff that trumps your existing tariff.

Shopping around for contents insurance

The insurance market is also a competitive one. Do not accept the premiums you have to pay just because you paid it last year. Get in contact with a good insurance broker to get the best deal.

Have you ever considered not getting insurance? Sometimes you can pay a hefty premium to insure very little – and even then you don't get a payout when you make a claim.

Purchasing second-hand furniture

What's more important to you – owning a house or owning nice furniture? If you are serious about wanting to own your own house,you will do whatever it takes to do it. This may mean sitting on a second-hand sofa, sleeping on an old bed and eating off a table your cousin gave you!

There are many incentives: retailers offer such things as 0% finance, buy now pay later, bank holiday one-off sales, etc. Do not be tempted! Save the cash now and get the new furniture later. Once you've bought your flat or house you can start thinking of furnishing it properly.

Travel

Selling the car

Owning and running a car is not cheap. You've got HPI payments, insurance premiums, road tax duty, petrol and oil costs, servicing costs and repairs. That's a lot of expenses! You could save a small fortune if you did sell the car.

Do a feasibility test on the car. Work out how much you spend a month on the car and see if it is greater than if you walked, cycled, took the train or bus or took taxis. If it is it's time to sell the car. Remember a car is a luxury item. Public transport is supposed to be getting better and providing better value for money, so be brave – get rid of it!

Downsizing the car

It may not be practical to get rid of the car but you could downsize it:

■ Consider a smaller car with a smaller engine – this will cut fuel costs.

■ Consider a lower insurance grouped car. Even consider third-party only insurance. When was the last time you had an accident? Statistically you are unlikely to have an accident that is your fault if you haven't had an accident in the last five years.

■ Maybe you could sell the car on HPI and buy a cheap run-around, thus saving on the loan repayments.

■ Road tax is reduced by £60 per year if you drive a car of less than 1.5 litres.

■ Get the car serviced by a non-main dealer.

Walking or getting a bike!

If you don't have a car but get buses, trains and/or taxis, consider walking or cycling. You will save on the fares *and* it will keep you fit!

Entertainment and clothing

Shopping in the sales, markets and charity shops

A good friend of mine's dad told me he buys his winter suits in summer and his summer suits in winter. The key is to get value for money. If you're shopping in a glitzy, air-conditioned, fashionable part of town you are paying for it. All the expenses they have to meet are ultimately paid by you because they charge a high mark-up on the goods they sell.

You'll be surprised how well stocked some of the market traders are. I still get most of my designer clothes from markets and superstores – not New Bond Street in London W1!

Thinking about whether it's a need or a want

As mentioned above, you need always to ask yourself if it's a need or a want. Do you really need to see the latest releases at the cinema or can you wait a year when they hit the Sky channels? Is the latest Kylie CD single with all the mixes really necessary or can you wait for her album? Do you really need the extra pair of trousers that are half price in the sale or are you buying them because they're cheap? If you master this thought process alone then half the battle is won.

Not staying out late

I find that, when I stay out later, I spend more. More on drinks, food, taxis and club entrances. Go home early! I'm not saying just stay out for an hour or so but try to arrive early and to go home early. You'll find that you come home with some cash in your pocket rather than having to revisit the cash machine on the night out and regretting it later!

Looking out for the deals bars, clubs, cinemas and restaurants offer

The entertainment industry is highly competitive. Virtually every evening spot has an offer. Take advantage of this. Look out for flyers or leaflets at their premises. Scan the local press for a restaurant trying to drum up a bit more business. Pay close attention to the TV ads to find out when Pizza Hut and other restaurant chains are doing a promotion.

Loans and savings plans

Switching credit cards and loans to obtain the best deals

Does 0% APR for balance transfers sound familiar? I'm sure you've heard this so many times that it no longer means anything – but it does! It means you can save a lot of cash as you pay no interest on your borrowing. Make sure you capitalise on these deals to save you real money. But don't just be happy with saving money – make an effort to clear these balances. You will run out of credit companies eventually, so you do need to clear this type of unhealthy borrowing.

Cashing in or freezing payments to endowment policies and pension plans

Is the endowment policy you are contributing to really going to mature to its estimated value? You could cash it in, raise cash and save cash as you no longer need to contribute to it.

It's the same for pension contributions. You could freeze payments, which will result in an instant saving. When I used to work I was tempted to contribute to a pension but, after careful thought, I realised that under no circumstances was I going to hand over any of my hard-earned cash to a company that would 'play' with it on the stock market. I did not want to be unsure of how much I would get back and not have access to it until I was of retirement age.

If you want a real pension fund, invest in property. But that's another story – or even another book!

Raising Your Initial Investment

Apart from saving the income you currently earn, there are other quick ways of raising the initial investment required to start your business. How much you need to raise will depend on the business you decide to run but, below, is a list of different ways of raising cash quickly. The following are in the order of the 'cost' to you, starting with the cheapest, the cost is the effective interest rate paid on the initial investment. (BoE means current Bank of England base rate.)

Personal Assets

(Cost: 0%) These are assets that are no longer being used but that have some resale value. This may be jewellery, cars, furniture, pieces of art, electrical equipment, etc. The cost is nil as the assets are not being used, but they could be used to realise some cash in order to invest. Look in the garage or attic – you may be surprised! Think about it like this: you're trading in your Ford now for the Ferrari in five years' time!

Savings

(Cost: BoE base rate) You may have savings in a deposit account or cash ISA. If you use this money the cost will be the lost interest that would have been earned if you had left it in the account.

Endowment policies or company shares

(Cost: BoE base rate + 3%) You could surrender an endowment policy or liquidise a current share portfolio to raise the cash. I recommend you talk to your financial adviser and stock broker before taking this action as you could be better off holding on to some of these policies or shares. However, it could be time to let go of some poorly performing stocks and enter the property arena as so many share market investors are now doing.

The cost of this, on average, is equivalent to the average return the stock market delivers. This, of course, will be different depending on the type of policy or stocks you hold. You could be better off if you sell now as they could result in a loss in the future.

Borrowing from the family

(Cost: BoE + 4%) You may have a family member who has cash sitting in the bank and who is willing to lend it to you. You can offer this person a better rate of return than any deposit account could. If they are a close member of the family, they might lend it to you for 0%, but if you proposition a family member offering BoE + 4%, you might get quite a few more positive responses than you expected.

You could access your inheritance early, as many families do, to avoid inheritance tax. As long as the donor lives seven years beyond the date of the gift there is no inheritance tax to pay, and is thus beneficial to both parties. A family member may be more willing to give you assets if you are proposing to invest them further rather than just squandering it on a new car or holiday.

Secured borrowings

(Cost: BoE + 2–7%) To do this you must already own a property. The cheapest way to do this is to remortgage the whole property and release the equity tied up in your home. It pays to shop around. A good mortgage broker could probably beat the rate you are currently paying and even might reduce your monthly payments while still raising some cash.

The other way is to get a second-charge loan where you keep your existing mortgage and borrow on the remaining equity on the house. You've probably seen the TV ads promising you a new car or holiday just from one phone call. Well, forget a new car or holiday – we're going into business!

Unsecured borrowings

(Cost: BoE + 2–15%) The cheapest way to do this is to transfer a current credit card balance to a new credit card with introductory rate offers. You draw out as much cash as you can on your current credit card and then apply for a credit card that has a low introductory rate for balance transfers until the balance is cleared. Once your new credit card has been approved, you transfer your existing balance on your old credit card to the new credit card at the introductory rate, typically BoE + 2%. This rate is fixed until you clear the balance.

You may, however, not get this new credit card. The other way is to draw down the cash on your existing credit card at the credit card rate. This can be expensive but, if your business has guaranteed customers, you could use the cash on a short-term basis, say one to two years, and use the profits to clear the credit card balance over that period.

You may be able to arrange an overdraft or a personal loan with your bank at around BoE + 6%. You need to speak to your bank manager.

You can also go to other unsecured lenders but there are high arrangement fees and the interest rate can even go up to BoE + 35%! You need to shop around but I would advise steering clear of anything with an interest rate higher than 25% unless you are really desperate and the business idea is a dead cert.

Getting a partner

(Cost: Varies) The other way to raise the cash is by taking on a financial partner. This means the financial risk is borne by the partner but you end up doing all the work. The partner will be entitled to a share of your profits, and you will not be free to do what you want with the business. The cost to you will depend on how successful the business is as the cost will be a share of the profits made. Even though this is the most expensive way to finance a business it can also be the cheapest if the whole project fails as your partner has taken the full financial risk. If this is the only method you can use to get into business I would still advise taking on a partner as you will still be freeing yourself from the rat race.

This is not an exhaustive list. You may have other good ideas for raising finance but, if you can't raise the finance, the project can't go ahead. It's as simple as that. I raised my initial investment by saving as much of my salary as I could. While my colleagues were spending everything they earned on high rents on apartments, expensive holidays and designer clothes, I saved my money by living in one room in a shared house, holidaying in the UK and wearing unbranded clothes. After five years I live in a large detached house with a swimming pool, holiday abroad three times a year and wear only designer clothes. You need patience and a medium to long-term vision if you truly desire to have enough wealth to live the lifestyle you want.

Maintaining Your Fixed Costs of Living

In an ideal world, as soon as you go in to business it will make a profit and these profits will maintain your fixed costs of living. However, we live in a less than ideal world and it is likely that you will make a loss in the first year – but your fixed costs of living still have to be met. So how do you raise this short-term cash? It can come from three sources, and the order of these three sources is as follows:

1. First, you
2. then family and friends
3. then outside agencies.

Let's look at this in more detail.

You

Going part-time at work

Leaving the rat race could be a two-stage process. If it is possible to go part time in your current job and implement your business in the other time, then you can see how well your business is doing. Once your business is up and running and providing you with a satisfactory income, you can leave work completely.

Getting a flexible part-time job

If you can get a job that doesn't require you to be in at a certain time or can be done during hours that won't affect the setting up of your business, your fixed costs can be maintained. Examples of this type of job are proofreading, handicraft jobs or parcel deliveries, where you get paid on an hourly basis, or flexible jobs where you work for bursts of time, such as temping, strawberry picking or taxi driving.

Do not get on your high horse and say these jobs are beneath you. You only have to do them while you are setting up. Once your business takes off you can take pride in the fact that you did these jobs.

Around three years ago when I was setting up, I took on two weeks' work for an accountancy firm even though I was escaping from the rat race of an accountancy firm. But I knew this job was necessary for me to pay my bills! It was only for two weeks in the year and in fact I quite enjoyed my time with this firm. I was paid £100 per day which, at the time, was quite needed. Now I charge £100 per hour but I would not be in this position if I had been too proud to take on this ad hoc work in the past.

Getting a complementary job
What better way to find out what it would be like to run a business than to go to work for a firm in that type of business? If your idea is to run a restaurant, go get a job in a restaurant. You will acquire certain insider tricks and tips and also get a real feel as to what it would be like to run that type of business.

This strategy has two benefits. It pays your bills and helps you find out whether that business is the right one for you.

Family and friends

Gifts
As I mentioned earlier, you will be surprised by the support you might get from the people around you. Now, I'm not saying go round all your family and friends with a begging bowl but, if your

family and social circle know what you are doing, they may well move forward certain cash gifts they were planning.

A family member of mine gave me £5,000 in cash to invest as it was in any case going to be left to me upon their death. They considered that it was better to give it to me now as I needed it and would double it in a short period of time. In fact it can be very tax efficient if your family members do give you your cash early as you can avoid inheritance tax in certain circumstances (usually when the deceased has more than £259,000 to leave). Please seek professional advice for more details.

Loans

In certain cultures, such as Jewish and Asian, it is commonplace to borrow from friends. Personally I have never done this even though I am Asian, but if you are part of a tightknit community and you know people who trust you, why not ask? They can only say 'no!'

Ad hoc work

Use your contacts. If you can get a family member or friend to get you a short-term job in between setting up your business, then get it! It's essential you keep up with your bills and know that you can get a quick income by picking up the phone and doing an odd day's work.

Outside agencies

Loans

This is not the ideal way to fund your fixed costs of living but it is one way. If you are thinking of taking out a loan try to get 12 months' worth of your shortfall, and try to pay it off over the longest period possible. This way your monthly loan repayments are kept to a minimum.

If you can, try to get a loan that does not penalise you if you pay it off early. This means that, if your business takes off earlier than expected, you can redeem the debt when you want, thus saving on interest.

Overdrafts

Overdrafts are more suitable as they can be paid off as and when you wish to. Apply for an overdraft facility *before* you leave work as your bank is unlikely to give you the facility once you've left work as you have no provable income. The great thing about overdrafts is that you only pay interest on the balance outstanding and on a daily basis. If the business does well at the start, the overdraft can be redeemed sooner than planned.

When I left work I had a £10,000 overdraft facility in place. I let it run up to around £5,000 before business picked up, but I was thankful I had such a facility.

Credit cards

I don't care what people might say about credit cards – they are great! It's those cardholders who do not know how to use them who have given them a bad name. One of my current credit card providers offered me £10,000 in cash at 0.7% APR for four months – so I took it! I will use it to fund property purchases and then redeem it in time when one of my remortgages comes through.

As long as you have a plan to repay the credit card company within a set period of time, there is no speedier way of raising cash than a credit card – and precisely when you need it.

As you can see from the above you have to mature in the way you handle cash, be active in raising cash and be inventive when it comes to raising cash quickly. This is crucial to running a business and ensuring it survives. Many business gurus will tell you this one phrase: 'cash is king'. It doesn't really matter where the cash comes from as long as you can pay your debts when they fall due so that you remain in business. The definition of insolvency (in other words, bankruptcy) is when the debtor is unable to pay his or her debts in full *and* on time. So to remain in the black you always have to have access to cash – quickly!

So you've learned how to preserve, earn and raise cash. Next you have to decide what you are going to do with it. You need to invest it: you need to identify what business you are going to run. Step 3 helps you to do just that.

Step 3
Deciding What
to Do

Identifying the Right Business for You

Identifying the right business might be easy if you already have an idea of what you want to do. If, like most, you don't have an idea it can be very difficult to home in on an idea you truly believe in. Who are you? Who you are is very important in deciding which type of business you want to get in to. *You* are the only person responsible for running *your* business. I have come up with three methods that should direct you away from certain businesses and, more importantly, direct you towards a business that suits you and will result in success.

The three methods I have created are:

1. elimination and choice
2. dissection
3. supply chain.

The key to finding your true vocation is to use all three methods. You are looking for prompts, hints and 'light-bulb moments' to trigger an idea that will inspire you enough to leave the rat race.

Elimination and Choice Method

So, how do you identify the right business for you? This is a two-stage process of elimination and choice. Look at Figure 1. You will see that you have to home in on the business that is suitable for you by eliminating certain businesses and then choosing from the rest. We'll look at these two processes in more detail.

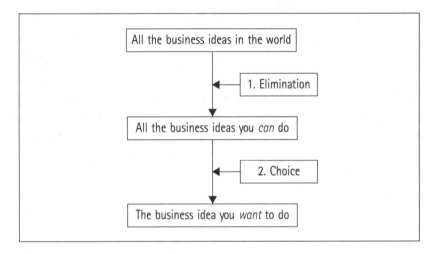

Fig. 1. Elimination and choice.

Elimination

The following factors are key in eliminating certain businesses from the equation.

Your ability

There's no point in trying to start a business that you are unable to do. While there are obvious examples, such as trying to set up your own solicitor practice when you're not a solicitor, there are also subtler examples, such as trying to set up your own PR agency when you hate speaking on the phone.

Think about your weaknesses. Are there businesses you would like to set up but after some careful thought you realise that you aren't able to run those businesses in the first place? Are there certain skills you simply don't have and are unlikely to acquire? Do you have any disabilities which will prevent you from doing certain things?

On the flipside think about your strengths. Do you have personal attributes that seem well suited to certain businesses? Do you have certain qualifications that put you at an advantage? If so, then keep these businesses in.

Is it feasible?

You might have an idea that has never been tested before. So the key question you have to ask yourself is – is it feasible? To answer this question you have to think through the idea thoroughly. What are the costs involved? What's the likely demand for your product or service? Will this idea make enough money for you to live on? You can get closer to the answers to these questions by drawing up forecasts, talking to people and, if possible, test marketing your idea.

If your preliminary research proves that the idea seems feasible, keep it in; if not, throw it out.

Location

If you have to live in a particular area because of family, friends or simply because you love living there, there will be a restriction on the businesses you can run. If you want to open up a bar or nightclub, for example, but there is a glut of these types of business in your area this idea has to be eliminated. All the businesses that can only be run outside of this area also have to be eliminated.

Is it realistic?

The ideas you can consider have to be realistic. If you are thinking of opening up a chain of supermarkets but you only have £1,000 to start up with, your idea is very unrealistic. If you have £1 million then your idea suddenly becomes realistic.

Think about whether or not you have realistic expectations of what business you can do based on your starting capital.

Choice

So you have eliminated most of your ideas but not all of them. Out of the remaining ideas you have to choose one. You should take the following factors into consideration when choosing.

Your interests

This alone can make or break your business. You have to be interested in what you are considering doing – any successful businessperson will tell you this. Do you believe in the proposed product or service? Is the business you are considering something your mind naturally wanders to?

There is no point in getting into something you think will bore you. Remember, you are trying to leave the rat race, not join another one!

Strategic fit

This takes into consideration your existing networks of people. You will be surprised what skills, information and expertise they have if you spend the time to think about it. Do you have a friend or family member who is in a job or business that is complementary to your business idea? Can you obtain vital information or secure preferential terms from this person that will help your business? For example, you're considering starting a plumbing business and your uncle owns a portfolio of properties. You could approach him offering your services. As he's your uncle he'll probably take you up on your proposition – I hope!

Dissection Method

This is a simple case of dissecting the market into two and deciding which side you want to be in. If you repeat this process you will eventually home in to the market you wish to be in. However, there are infinite ways of dissecting the market. The following are the key dissections to get you started.

Retail v. trade

Retail is selling directly to the public. This is often known as B2C (business to consumer), where the customer is the eventual end user of your product. Trade is selling directly to another business: B2B (business to business) where your product forms part of the final product that is eventually sold to the consumer. The most important differences between these approaches are are as follows:

- B2C needs many customers; B2B doesn't.

- B2C needs a more sophisticated after-sales customer care; B2B doesn't.

- B2C requires lots of marketing; B2B doesn't.

- B2C requires a shopfloor; B2B doesn't.

If you want to be in retail you must be willing to accept the mantra – 'the customer is always right'. If you don't you could find yourself in the latest episode of *Watchdog* and very quickly out of business. If you want to be in trade you must be very cost efficient as your business customers will be very cost focused.

I personally like being in the trade sector as the public can be very fickle. You can come across a customer who causes so many problems they end up wasting hours of your time. However, if you really do understand the public in your targeted market, the rewards can be very high.

Passive v. active

Passive businesses earn income from investments. This could be property, intellectual property, royalties, stocks, bonds or anything else that does not require your effort. You acquire these investments by putting in your own cash, the bank's cash or by having a financial partner. This concept is that you use money (or borrowed money) to make money – true capitalism!

Active businesses earn income from direct labour effort. This could be a solicitor, plumber, mechanic, consultant or any other business that requires you to provide a service or product.

If you're looking to free up time to spend with your family or friends or you're simply lazy, passive businesses are the most suitable. If you're someone who gets bored easily when you have free time or you are unwilling to borrow heavily, active businesses are the most suitable.

Services v. manufacturing

The service sector has no tangible product. It provides businesses or consumers with the wherewithal to achieve certain goals. Typical service sector businesses are broking, travel agencies and repairers.

The manufacturing sector produces tangible products. Examples are computer and clothing manufacturers and craft industries.

Do you get great pleasure out of creating a product? Or do you get greater pleasure out of putting your time and effort into providing a service?

Trading v. investing

A trader will buy something and sell it on within a year. An investor will buy something and hold on to it for longer than a year. A typical trader is a business such as a supermarket, car dealer or market trader. These businesses simply buy and then sell. A typical investor is such a business as the renting of properties or the investing of stocks and shares. These businesses buy and then hold to obtain a continual stream of income. It is possible to do both. You could, for example, buy properties or stocks to hold *and* trade but, usually, people do one or the other.

I personally consider myself an investor. When you invest you can be assured of a continual stream of income for the time you hold on to the investment. I invest because I am then not always on the lookout for the next deal. With trading you have to ensure that you can always find a supplier who delivers the right goods at an attractive price.

Low v. high capital requirement

This is an important dissection as the threshold for what counts as high and low is subjective. Assuming it's £10,000, you can dissect businesses into the categories of those that require less than £10,000 to start and more than £10,000. The starting capital you can raise will determine which sector you can be in.

If all you can raise is £1,000 there is no point in thinking about opening your own pub unless you are willing to take on a financial partner. If you have £50,000, opening your own pub could be a reality.

Inventive v. existing

Do you want to run your own restaurant or do you want to write an inventive piece of software? If you are a creative person you may wish to operate a business that pushes the boundaries. These businesses are higher risk and usually fail but, if you get it right, the rewards are massive. If you are more conventional and prefer to tread a tried and tested route, the existing sector may be more suitable. There are, however, still opportunities to be creative within the existing sector.

Outside v. inside

Do you like the outdoors or do you like staying indoors? Is the thought of being in an office too much to bear but being out on a building site seems more natural? Whatever your preference you can decide your environment – it's your business!

Old v. new economy

There was once a big hype about how internet businesses (the new economy) would come to dwarf traditional businesses (the old economy). This led to frantic investment in half-baked Internet ideas with barely a single business plan. Lots of investors got their fingers burnt, and now Internet business ideas always carry a stigma. However, there are many good ideas that can be implemented with a little cash and labour power.

Do you fear computers or do you only ever imagine working with them? Depending on your preference you can decide how hi-tech you want to be. No matter what people say, you can still run a business without having to go near a computer – it's your choice.

This is not a complete list. Think about other ways to dissect the market and consider which side you wish to be in. Based on your preferences from the dissections above, you can build up a profile. A typical profile might look like Table 1.

Table 1. Example profile.

Dissection	Profile
Retail v. trade	Retail
Passive v. active	Active
Services v. manufacturing	Services
Trading v. investing	Trading
Low v. high capital requirement	Low
Inventive v. existing	Existing
Outside v. inside	Inside
Old v. new economy	Old

Using this profile you can think about different businesses. In this example possible businesses you could do are:

- mortgage broker
- mobile motor mechanic
- freelance caterer.

Supply Chain Method

This final method involves choosing an industry you are interested in and then thinking of all the products and services that make up that industry. After considering these products and services you can decide if anything takes your interest.

This is best explained by the following example. Dave loves to skateboard. The industries surrounding skateboarding are shown in Figure 2.

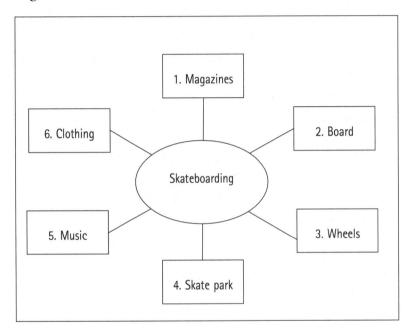

Fig. 2. The industries surrounding skateboarding.

The options Dave has to choose between are as follows:

1. **Magazines**.
   Dave could consider whether he would like to be a freelance writer, photographer or researcher for an existing magazine. He could think a little higher and start his own magazine. There might, for example, be a gap in the market where there are no UK magazines, only magazines imported from the USA.

Or there might be a niche in the magazine market that hasn't been tapped, such as a dedicated speed-skating magazine.

2. **Board**.

   All skateboarders need a skateboard! One of the key parts of a skateboard is the board itself. Dave could consider designing artwork for the boards themselves. Or he could set up a skateboard shop which sold many differently designed boards, including his own.

3. **Wheels**.

   As well as needing a board you need the wheels. Again, he could set up as a retailer of specialised wheels. He could get involved in the research, design and testing of the ultimate frictionless wheel if he had the experience and qualifications.

4. **Skate park**.

   You need somewhere to skate! There are skate parks all over the country, and Dave could get involved in the design, construction, fund-raising and promotion of the park on a freelance basis.

5. **Music**.

   Skaters have very definitive music. Dave could become a DJ at certain venues dedicated to skaters. He could get involved with the production of the music and set up his own record label. He could run his own skater nights at nightclubs and at skate parks.

6. **Clothing**.

   Skaters have very distinctive clothing. Dave could get involved in the retailing of this clothing. He could also consider making these garments or designing them, depending on his skills.

As you can see, lots of ideas can be generated from one industry if you think of the other industries that surround it. I must stress that when you think of an industry choose one you are interested in! It will then be more likely that you will come up with an idea in a related industry you are not only interested in but, more importantly, also believe in.

Step 4
Jack in the Job

Overcoming Your Fears and Leaving Your Job

Paradoxically, this is one of the hardest as well as one of the easiest things to do. It's hard because:

■ very few people do it;

■ you don't know many people who have done it;

■ you've never done it;

■ it results in change; and

■ it's the unknown.

It's easy because:

■ it makes sense!

Hopefully, if you agree with what was said in the previous chapters you now see the opportunities involved in leaving employment. If you have done the preparation, the risks you face should be manageable. However, if you are a normal breathing human you still have that thing called *fear*. Let's examine this fear to see how we can best eliminate it so you can ultimately leave your job.

The Fears Involved In Leaving Your Job

There are a number of fears people have about leaving their jobs that are fully justified. They are not dissimilar to what business people face when appraising a potential investment. These are called risks. The difference between an ordinary person and a business person is that a business person:

- identifies all the risks involved;

- mitigates each risk as best they can;

- considers the overall risk based on how well they can mitigate each individual risk; and

- makes a decision based on the overall risk.

So to leave your job you need to:

- identify all the fears involved in leaving your job;

- think how you can overcome each fear involved in leaving your job;

- consider the overall fear factor based on how well you can overcome each individual fear; and

- decide whether you want to leave your job or not based on the overall fear factor.

Fortunately for you, I'm not going to ask you to think of all your fears – you probably know most of these already. Instead, I'm going to tell you how to overcome these fears and calculate the overall fear factor. Unfortunately for you, I'm not going to decide

for you whether you should leave your job because I am not you!
However, I will present a very strong case and I will recommend
that you leave – but the ultimate decision rests with you.

The Fears and Overcoming Them

The following are the seven most common fears:

1. *Defaulting on your financial commitments.*
   I think this the biggest fear of them all. When we start work
   we start to get a taste for material things. When we can't
   afford the things we want we buy things using not only the
   money we have now but also the money we will earn in the
   future. Basically, we buy things on credit: things like houses,
   cars, furniture and other expensive items. We get used to
   these items and think that we could never do without them.

   The thought of doing without them is such a fearful thought it
   keeps you working till you are at least 60. It is only natural
   that the mental picture you associate with leaving your job is
   the loss of your material goods. It threatens yours and your
   family's place in society, expulsion from your current social
   circle and exposure to less than desired situations, such as an
   increased risk of becoming the victim of crime.

2. *Loss of social contact.*
   Time spent with work colleagues may dwindle to nothing as
   the majority of the time you see them is at work. You may be
   able to maintain relationships but you feel left behind as the
   others still spend time together at work.

3. *Disappointment of family and friends.*
   No matter if you are in a dead end job, you will still have the disappointment of certain family members and friends to contend with. They will question your attitude and responsibility to yourself and your dependants. They will wonder what the hell you are doing!

4. *Loss of status resulting in loss of respect and sexual appeal.*
   If you're a manager, director, doctor, investment banker or any other job that gives you credibility, responsibility or status, then leaving your job will take this away. You will miss the control, power and respect you command over others, which all contribute to your self-esteem.

5. *Loss of security.*
   The security of future income is lost. The money you will be earning in the future is unknown. It's this unknown that fills you with fear and insecurity. With a job your future income can be charted with some degree of accuracy.

6. *Going without the normal luxuries of life.*
   You fear you will lose out on your leisure activities, good food, stylish clothes and nights out with your friends as you won't be able to afford to. Having a job allows you to have a certain degree of freedom when it comes to spending money because you have money!

7. *Unable to cope mentally.*
   The stress that comes with leaving your job, running a business and being totally responsible for the amount of money that comes in to the household may be too much to cope with.

For every fear you can take **countermeasures** that overcome each fear. A countermeasure is an action you take to counteract each fear. However, no countermeasure is foolproof, otherwise a fear would not be a fear because it can be overcome.

There will still always be a remnant of fear, albeit a lot less than the initial fear. This is what I call *residual fear*. A residual fear is therefore still present even after the countermeasure and is, thus, is a real fear. You can take further countermeasures to reduce this residual fear but this depends on how far you want to go.

No matter what you do, however, there will always be a residual fear. A fear that cannot be eliminated is that you will ultimately go bankrupt. This is faced by every business in the world as this is the very nature of business. If this fear did not exist we would all be self-employed! But remember that your employer faces this fear too and if they were to go bankrupt, you would be out of a job and you too could also go bankrupt. The possible fears, countermeasures and residual fears in leaving your job are presented as Table 2.

Overall Fear

To calculate your overall fear, you need to gather all your residual fears. To do this you should:

- decide which fears listed in the table are fears you actually have;
- decide what countermeasures you are willing to take for each fear; and
- calculate the residual fear for each applicable fear.

Table 2. Fears, countermeasures and residual fears.

Fear	Countermeasures	Residual fear	Further countermeasures
1. Defaulting on your financial commitments	If you've followed the previous steps you should have: • minimised your financial commitments to a manageable level; and • arranged suitable finance to maintain these financial commitments for a period of 12 months	The finance you have arranged to maintain these commitments runs out	You have arranged emergency finance from: • being willing to work part time; • friends and family; or • loans, overdrafts or credit cards
2. Loss of social contact	Maintaining the friendships you have with your work colleagues. This means making the effort to see them when it suits them	The friendships still dwindle away even though you make the effort	Being open minded to making new friends who might lead a similar lifestyle to yours
3 Disappointment from family and friends	Explaining to each person exactly what you are doing and why	They still do not approve	Realise that you are the most important person and that living the 9–5 rat race will lead you to an early grave. You must muster up the confidence to do this for yourself and you must realise that the others around you will understand when you succeed

Fear	Countermeasures	Residual fear	Further countermeasures
4 Loss of status resulting in the loss of respect and sexual appeal	Understanding that status is really all about self-importance. If you rely on it, it masks a deeper insecurity about yourself	Still feel less respected and sexually appealing	None!
5 Loss of security	Understanding that life is unpredictable even if you have a job! If you've followed all the steps in this book you will make your business work, and the only thing that is unpredictable is whether you make a lot or loads!	You feel secure about the near future but worry about the mid to long-term future	You understand that you will work as hard as you can to ensure you have enough investments to look after you in the long term
6 Going without the normal luxuries of life	Understanding that, if you go without now, you will have ten times more in the future	You are left wondering what it's all about if you can't even have a few little luxuries	Allowing yourself a planned treat every now and again as long as it doesn't blow your budget!
7 Unable to cope mentally	Try to remember what it's like to get up early in the morning and drag yourself to work for eight solid hours, knowing that what you are going through doesn't compare	A residual stress still remains	Understanding that nothing lands in your lap. You have to undergo a degree of stress to free yourself from stress

Fear	Countermeasures you are willing to take	Residual fear
1. Default on your financial commitments	• Minimise financial commitments so you have a manageable level prior to leaving your job • Arrange 12 months' finance to cover these commitments • Willing to work part time if need be	You default on your financial commitments when your 12 months' finance runs out and you can't get a part-time job that is sufficient to meet all your costs
3. Disappointment of family and friends	• Explain to all what you are doing • Knowing that staying in the rat race will kill you	None
4. Loss of status resulting in loss of respect and sexual appeal	• Realise that status is all about self-importance. You will meet someone who will appreciate your status	Loss of sexual appeal
6. Going without the normal luxuries of life	• None	Going without life's luxuries
7. Unable to cope mentally	• Willing to work hard • Having the constant reminder that leaving your job is better than staying	None

Table 3. Totalling your overall fear.

So, for example, if you had the fears shown in Table 3 and were willing to take the suggested countermeasures, your overall fear is the contents of the residual fear column.

The overall fear, therefore, is the total of the residual fear:

- You default on your financial commitments when your 12 months' finance runs out and you can't get a part-time job that is sufficient to meet all your costs.

- Loss of sexual appeal.

- Going without life's luxuries.

You have to estimate the likelihood of these things happening and whether the rewards from starting your own business are strong enough to compensate for them. If you are happy with this overall fear, you will leave your job and start a business. If you are not, you won't. If you are not happy with the overall fear I suggest you take more countermeasures so that your overall fear is reduced. Once you reduce it to a level you are happy with, leaving your job becomes a simple and obvious thing to do.

Step 5
Getting Started

Implementing the Business of Your Choice

If you've followed Step 4 then I can say welcome – welcome to freedom. You will not regret it. This is where life begins. Now you need to channel your passion and energy into starting your very own business. In summary you need, loosely and in this order, to do the following:

1. Get the tools.

2. Educate yourself.

3. Promote your business.

4. Inform the authorities.

5. Control the cash.

6. Understand your competitors.

7. Understand your customers.

8. Build alliances.

Get The Tools

You must have the tools you need to run your business from the start. Now, this will depend on what type of business you are doing but you need the tools to provide the service or product. The key word is *need*. While it's nice to have a fax machine, computer and attractive personal assistant, are these necessary if your choice of business is to become a builder? The more cash you can save in these early days the better.

There are certain tools you will need but it is up to you to decide whether they are necessary or not. My advice is that, if you are in doubt about whether you need it or not, forget it. If you can preserve cash by not buying unnecessary tools, do so. You can always acquire it if you do need it. But how do you decide whether it's necessary?

Office equipment

This includes telephone, fax, computer, printer and anything else found in an office. Some of this can be very expensive. Where you can, avoid getting the latest technology as you'll find the older outdated models do the same thing but just a bit slower. The number of times I have seen people buying a £2,000 laptop, justifying the expense because they say they need it to go into business, only to find they have just £1,500 left to invest.

If you're thinking of running a business that requires minimal paperwork consider whether any office equipment is necessary at all. You'll be surprised how far pen and paper go. Acquiring office equipment may make you feel like you're in business but its worth might be limited and it could drain your cash just when it's most needed.

Office space

Office space is expensive. You really only need office space if you are going to have clients coming to your premises. Otherwise the spare room, a corner in your living room or even your garage or shed will suffice. I still operate from my home and I know of many other self-employed people who do.

Stationery

Getting fancy business cards, invoices and compliment slips may make you think you're in business but it's when you make your first sale that you know you really are in business. If you are in a market where your letterhead is a key 'calling card', then invest in a good letterhead. If you're in a business where your image is a key representation of your firm, invest in a good suit. Have the sense to know whether fancy stationery will drum up business or not.

Car or van

I knew a guy who wanted to start a property business about 100 miles from where he lived. The crazy thing was he didn't know how to drive. I'm not sure how he expected to go from one property to the other but, if he had spent his cash on taxis, he would have eroded his profit to nothing.

Evaluate whether you need transport. In some businesses it is obvious whether you need a car; others are not so obvious. Running a car is expensive, as mentioned earlier, but if it's necessary, get one. There's nothing more frustrating than knowing you have a customer waiting but you can't get there.

Information sources

If your business demands you have access to certain trade journals, websites or newsletters, subscribe to them. Factor this cost in your plans as this information will be key to keeping abreast and ahead in the market.

I'm not suggesting you subscribe to all of them: speak to people in the industry. There will be a few primary, standard information sources everyone refers to.

Retail outlet

Depending on your business, you may need a shop or high-street outlet. This is expensive. Consider direct selling through mail order or the web and then progressing to a retail outlet.

Markets can be a great way to test market your product or service. You can get a stall on a week-by-week basis and these work out very cheap. If you do need a shop, consider approaching a shop and asking them to sell your product or service on a sale or return or commission basis.

Websites

Websites can either be cheap or expensive to set up – it depends on whom you go to or know. Consider whether your type of business demands a website. If you're going into the computer consultancy business, it would seem reasonable to set one up. If you're considering setting up a restaurant in a local part of town, the website can probably wait.

Registrations

If you need to be a member of a trade organisation to give your firm a certain degree of credibility, join it. If you are starting out you need all the credibility you can get. Make sure it is a credible organisation and not a Mickey Mouse one.

Employees

If your business idea needs immediate staff then start recruiting early. The right people can make or break you. Don't fall into the trap of employing the first person who comes along or, out of duty, a family member or friend who has just been made redundant.

Listings

Be sure to contact *Yellow Pages*, *Thomson* and 192 (or 118 118 as it is now called) enquiries to get a listing. You will be surprised how many calls you will receive if you are in a niche business. This is *free*. Do not be tempted to pay for an advert in any of these directories as they are hugely expensive. Once you're established think about it. Remember – you need all the cash you've got; don't squander it!

This is not an exhaustive list; there are other primary tools depending on what type of business you are considering. Carefully evaluate whether they are necessary now or whether they can wait until you are more established. Do not make the mistake of ploughing all your capital into primary tools if you have no idea whether you're going to be in business in the next six months as you've not even had your first order.

Educating Yourself

This is very important. I have fallen foul of this. I entered in to the bar and nightclub business without any real understanding of the liquor trade. I am now learning and am still learning – the hard way! With hindsight I should have found out a lot more but the place was such a bargain I couldn't resist. To educate yourself you can do the following.

Chatting to people in the same industry

Whom better to speak to than someone in the industry? Make sure this person is not a potential competitor as they might mislead you. Ask to shadow this person, if possible, on a typical day.

Getting a book on it

If there are books on your proposed business, get them. The cost of a book is a tiny fraction of what you could lose if you don't follow the advice given. Also, there are many trade journals out there. If you can't afford to subscribe to them yet, see if you can borrow them from your local library.

Using the Internet

I don't have to tell you that the Internet is a great resource of information on anything – especially business.

Please, please, please do *not* go on expensive courses held in swanky hotels that tell you how you can make a fortune in such and such a business. The only businesses that can make you the kind of money they claim is the 'running expensive courses in swanky hotels' type of business! Everything you need can be found from the resources mentioned above. You don't need to spend hundreds or even thousands of pounds to be spoon fed basic information.

Promoting Your Business

It's no good starting a business unless you let people know about you. The way you do this is by promoting this fact.

You

The best promotional tool you have is *you*. You are the key representative of your business. Your ability to speak, act and deliver/carry out the business is paramount. The most effective way to promote your business is to do a good job. If it's done well, people will tell others: word of mouth is everything. If you say you are going to do something, then *do it*.

Working for nothing

If you believe that you are better than the rest then, initially, work for nothing. People will soon cotton on to the fact that you're better. Once you've proved yourself you can watch them come to you. A common trick is to do a job for a well-known company for a notional fee of £1. This way the company is technically a customer. You can then add this well-known customer to your list of satisfied customers, thus giving you credibility.

Free advertising

It's important at the start that you make use of all the free advertising you can get. This means telling everyone you are in business, putting your posters in the right places, targeting emails and getting press attention if you can.

Mailshots

One of my businesses was started from a mailshot. My accountancy practice was kick started by a targeted mailshot to 100 mortgage brokers offering my accountancy reference service. I received about six responses that resulted in work. Because I did a good job I was referred to other mortgage brokers and now my business grows from recommendations only.

If you think your business will get a positive boost from a targeted mailshot, do it. Get a good letterhead, quality paper and quality envelopes, and target your mailshot to prospective customers. Make sure your mailshot is well drafted. Run it by your friends and family or someone whose opinion you value.

Newspapers

Before spending a small fortune on a regular display advert in the local or national press, consider whom you are targeting. Many people read through a paper and don't even glance at the ads. If you're in a niche market, consider carefully if the mass press is suitable. Carefully selected trade magazines, newsletters and journals could be better and cheaper.

Leaflet drops

Leaflet drops save on postage. If you look at the cost of posting 1,000 leaflets at second-class rate it would total £200. If your business requires such mass marketing, such as a take-away or landscape gardening business, consider printing some cheap leaflets and delivering them *yourself*! Don't pay a child or school leaver to do it as you'll find three quarters of your leaflets in a bin or scattered all over the local playground.

Websites

As mentioned earlier, websites can be cheap to set up. If your business demands one make sure it's a good one. If you need one just as a calling card then get one and make sure you link it to as many search engines as possible.

I have a website and I get a call about once every two months as a result of this. I've never secured any business from it but I don't expect to. My business dictates that you must have a presence on the web but it's not crucial for gaining business. It really depends on your business. Consider whether your competitors have a website. If they don't then perhaps this could be a way of differentiating yourself from them.

Promotional discounts

If you do this right this can be a powerful promotional tool. If you're willing to supply your product or service at cost for the first few deals on each customer, do it. Once you've got them hooked you may have them for life.

Introduction fees

Another great way to build your business is to offer a commission to anyone who brings you in business. If I receive an introduction from someone I pay him or her 10% of what I get. This encourages your contacts to bring business to you as they know they're going to be paid.

Informing the Authorities

Not only do you have to let your potential customers know you're in business but you also have to inform the authorities. The following authorities will be interested in your new business venture:

Inland Revenue

Unfortunately we all have to pay tax. Write to your local Inland Revenue office, whose address can be found in *Yellow Pages*, to let them know you've started in business. They will write to you and send you a tax return to complete. You can fill this form out yourself or you can contact an accountant who will deal with it.

If you do use an accountant, shop around. You may not need a chartered or certified accountant as they will be expensive and their expertise may not be needed if you are running a small, uncomplicated business. A competent book-keeper may suffice and will be half the cost, if not cheaper.

The Inland Revenue will automatically inform the National Insurance Contributions Department who will then contact you to set up a £2 per week contribution from your bank. The rest of your NI contributions will be paid when you pay your tax.

VAT

If you expect your turnover to be greater than £15,000 per quarter you may have to get registered for VAT, depending on whether your product or service is subject to VAT. You will have to contact Customs & Excise to find out. Information about this and contact details can be found from their website *www.hmce. gov.uk*

Professional Bodies

In certain cases you need to inform the professional bodies that regulate your business. This includes the FSA for the financial industry, the Law Society for law, the Office of Fair Trading for a lending business or the ICAEW for chartered accountancy. There are many more so find out if your business is regulated. Non-registration can result in heavy fines and even imprisonment.

Controlling the cash

As I mentioned earlier, cash is king. That is why everything to do with the cash that comes in and out is the most important thing – *not the profit*. You pay bills with cash, *not* profit. Profit is a notional figure based on the agreed terms of your purchase and sale. However, if a customer defaults then the profit quickly turns into a loss.

Let's look at this in more detail.

Credit control

This is probably the most important side of the business when it comes to finances. If you can, never give credit. This may be impractical depending on what type of business you're in, but where you can do not give it. My accountancy practice demands payment upfront even though many accountants give credit. I don't care if I lose business by demanding this. If a customer doesn't want to pay upfront I would doubt whether they could pay at all.

If you do have to have debtors makes sure you keep tabs on them. Make it clear on your invoices when you expect payment (i.e. 'payment is required within 7 days of the date of this invoice'). If payment is not received on time have a system. It may be a phone call after one day, a letter after seven days and court action after a month.

Have credit limits for customers. Set it at zero for new customers rising to a figure that is no more than 10% of your working capital. Stay abreast of your customers' financial situations. If you know one of your customers is struggling consider reducing their credit limit. You don't want them going down and taking you with them.

Credit periods

While you should not give your customers credit try to get credit from your suppliers! This is simply the way business works. I know it doesn't seem fair but life's not fair. Wherever you can, get credit and take it. If you can get paid for a job before you've paid your supplier you've cracked it – you are generating cash without any cash! The only limit then on how much cash you can make will be purely the demand from your customers.

Pricing

Be sure to price your product or service correctly. Factor in unseen costs such as phone calls, postage, parking or any other cost that is not directly attributable to your product or service. You would be surprised how many people fall foul of this. They make a profit after variable costs (known as gross profit) but make a loss after all the overheads are taken into account (known as a net loss).

The best way to avoid this is to set your price by a technique known as skimming. Skimming is going in high and then shaving off a little bit if demand is low. You have to be competitive, though. If you are going to charge a higher price than your competitors you need to be offering something else, such as better after-sales care or a more robust product or service.

If your intention is to crush the competition by setting a low price, ensure you take into account the losses you may incur and how long you can sustain this for. If you do go in low, consider setting the prices higher than the competition for some of your range to compensate for this loss. This strategy is called loss leadership. It's the kind of strategy ASDA, Tesco and Sainsbury's use to crush the smaller supermarkets.

Budgeting

You do not need to go out to buy an expensive budgeting software pack so you can track every expenditure and calculate fancy statistics, but you must have an idea of what things cost. This is a game of money. Know how much *everything* costs and budget for it. You do not need any nasty surprises that catch you out and then put you out of business.

A calculation on a scrap of paper will suffice. Be sure to include every possible expense:

■ **Mobile phone calls**.
These can work out very expensive if you are calling cross-network.

■ **Postage**.
You'll be surprised how much a mailshot can cost if you send out over 500 letters.

■ **Printing**.
Ink cartridges for printers are set at a scandalous price. I pay £27 for a black ink cartridge which lasts me about two months. That's nearly £200 a year!

■ **Travel costs**.
Be sure to include parking costs, potential fines, extra servicing costs due to higher mileage, taxis and congestion charges.

■ **Bad debts**.
Some customers will not pay you – fact! I always budget 20% bad debt loss for my property business.

Understanding Your Competitors

It's not just you out there, you know. There are others doing exactly what you're doing – trying to make a living. The key thing is that you know who, what, why and where they are – and how and when!

Knowing who they are

Every business has competitors. If there's money to be made in a market there will always be several players fighting over a market share. If you are in the fortunate position to have no competitors (I can't think of a situation where this could occur, though), you can be sure there will be in the future. So know your competitors *and* potential competitors.

But why do we need to know who they are? We've all heard the expression 'keep your friends close and your enemies closer' but in business this is even more important. The competition are your enemies as they threaten your lifestyle. You need to know what they're up to and what their plans are. If you find you are losing business due to an introductory offer by one of your competitors, you will be able to react to it with full information.

Copying them

Now you've found out who they are, copy them! If you are struggling for inventive ideas, copy them. This is not illegal! You can use their ideas for inspiration or you can copy them and just make them better.

We see this happen all the time. McDonald's introduced the Value Meal and, shortly after, Burger King did the same. We had *Pop Idol* on ITV and *Big Brother* on Channel 4 and the BBC followed shortly with a combination of both in *Fame Academy*. They all add their little twist but essentially it's a copy of their competitor's ideas. There are no rules and regulations that govern the copying of ideas as this is what keeps businesses progressing.

Differentiating

If copying is not the best strategy then why not do something different? This may be offering something additional or offering a completely different product that does exactly the same thing. This requires you keeping up with the latest developments so that you know about products or practices that are more appealing or more efficient.

Branding is also a key way to differentiate. Easyjet, the low-cost airline, has succeeded in differentiating by offering just basic air travel without any frills. Their use of plain colours (orange and white) and the limited destinations nearly brought about the downfall of British Airways. British Airways tried fighting back with their copy, 'Go', but failed. Easyjet now offer a wider range of destinations and their only real threat is Ryan Air, another low-cost airline.

It is this differentiation that will make customers choose you over others. You must stand out. The worst thing for your business is that you blur into the rest and there is no solid reason why someone should choose you over others.

Consider differentiation by one of these means:

■ *Price*.
  Be at the top end or the bottom end of the market. Either be the cheapest with no frills or the most expensive with all the frills.

■ *Niche*.
  Be a specialist in one small part of the market, thus eliminating

most competitors. You can charge premium pricing for your expertise.

■ **Quality**.
Offer the best! People will come to you as you are offering the best in the market.

■ **After sales**.
You offer the best backup service for any issues arising after the purchasing of your product or service.

Understanding Your Customers

Knowing who they are

This seems obvious. You might be thinking: 'Well, I've sold to them so of course I know them'. What I'm saying is really *know* your customers: understand where they're heading and if your products or services will be required in the future. If so, be sure to guarantee a supply. If their requirements are going to change, change with them if possible.

Avoiding being reliant on a few

The classic way businesses go down is by a customer going down. If you only have a few customers your business is very fragile. You are reliant on the success of your few customers for your own success.

Tesco never relies on one customer; it has many – us! Their exposure is really thus the general UK economy. A pig farm, on the other hand, supplying meat exclusively to Tesco relies heavily on one customer: Tesco. If Tesco find another pig supplier at a cheaper price the original pig farm will ultimately go out of business.

Do whatever you can to minimise your exposure to one or just a few customers. Reread the section on promoting your business above to gain more customers.

Building Alliances

Building alliances is all about teaming up with non-competing businesses so you can sell one anothers' products and services. We've all heard about lastminute.com. The key to their success as the first Internet-site-based company in the UK to make a profit was their aggressive alliance programme. If you used the Internet or walked along the high street you would see lastminute.com somewhere. The great thing is that even if none of these alliances worked they still got their name out there alongside the 'big boys'. It just so happened that aligning themselves with household names made them a household name, which meant more hits to their website and, hence, more sales.

Depending on what your business is, there are many non-competing businesses that could sell your product or service and you theirs. You might also find that selling their products or services could be more profitable than selling your own.

Step 6
Don't Give Up

Persevering

Within 12 weeks you should have become accustomed to your new lifestyle. It will be a lifestyle of freedom. It will be a lifestyle you won't want to let go of. You'll be willing to do anything to preserve it. But it's no good saying 'I won't give up!' – you need to have a strategy that ensures that you *don't*.

I have come up with four methods you can use to ensure that you never give up. Again, use all the methods together to keep you motivated:

1. Fear and greed.

2. Negative-positive.

3. Competition.

4. Goal setting.

Fear and Greed

We all have drives. We are all driven to eat, sleep and to have sex. These are all actions that require no motivation as our bodies desire them without the need for conscious thought. Anything else requires motivation, including setting up and persevering with your own business. So how do you stay motivated? To be blunt we are all motivated to do things out of *fear* and out of *greed*.

I'm not saying you must be fearful and/or greedy as neither of these attributes are particularly nice. What you have to do is create the fear and the greed in your mind to motivate yourself. It's these feelings that will stop you procrastinating and drive you to do something! You need to be able to picture the fearful situation or the abundance that comes with greed.

It's up to you to create this fear and greed as what you fear and what you're greedy for will be based on your personal circumstances. Don't hold back – create the absolutely worst and best scenarios that will really motivate you. Here are some general ones to get you going.

Fear

Going back to the 9-5 grind
This is my biggest fear: it's not having enough money or time, just going back to work. I think I would rather go on the dole than go back to work. Remember what trap you've escaped from. Reread Step 1 if you've forgotten. As I was writing Step 1 it all came back. There is no way I'm going back to that.

Missing out on key events
There are certain events you will miss while you are at work. Simple things like the Football World Cup matches on TV or

extremely important things like hearing your child utter its first words.

Think of the pain you've felt because you were at work, missing out on things that are important to you.

Going out of business
Can you imagine the stress of going under? You will be a disappointment to your friends, family and, most importantly, to yourself. I know of businesspeople who have committed or attempted to commit suicide over this fear alone.

When you're struggling to keep motivated, think of the shame and embarrassment you will experience if you become lazy and let your business go down.

Working till you're too old to enjoy life
If you are employed you will work until at least the age of 55, and more likely, 65. There is so much I want to do before I hit 40! If I knew I would never have more than four weeks' holiday each year until I was 65 I think I would commit suicide!

Consider what you want to do and how employment would prevent you from doing it. It's surprising how many people work all their life and then die within two years of retirement. This is a strange phenomenon. It could be a result of the dramatic change from working for 40 years and then doing nothing. You feel worthless. Don't let this happen to you.

Greed

Never having to take orders from anyone

You can be the master of your own destiny. There are few people in this world who are in this privileged position. Whatever your situation is at any point in time is completely of your doing.

You will have no overbearing boss, no unachievable deadlines set by someone else, no extremely early or late starts and no boring meetings to sit through. This is because it's your business and you call the shots.

Having all the time in the world to do the really important things

What's important depends on you; only you decide on this. But whatever it is you can do it. If it's going to the park for the day or travelling round the world for six months, do it. If you've set your business up correctly it should be able to run itself.

Having enough money to buy anything you want

Just imagine being able to buy anything you want. Only successful entrepreneurs (and the royal family!) can buy anything that money can buy. You can only reach this position by setting up your own business.

Imagine you and your family having all the houses, cars, clothes, holidays and whatever else you and your family desire. You will have it but it all depends on how much you want it.

Having the peace of mind knowing that you are completely self-sufficient

No one's ever going to make you redundant: you have complete job security as you are your own employer. The threat of redundancy can only come from yourself. I am trying to make myself redundant through delegation: if I can get reliable people to run my business I will be able to do something else. All I will have to do is check my bank balance.

If the people who run my business turn out to be incompetent, they will be made redundant, not me. I will still have my business and I will just have to find better people.

Having an abundance of respect, adoration and accolade

If you want recognition the only way to achieve this is by being the owner. It's the owners who get the praise, adoration and accolade from the outside world – and rightly so! It was your idea and you took it to the market – that deserves a lot of respect.

Picture yourself on the front page of the business section of *The Times*, on TV telling people about your success story, on the radio promoting your product and at all those parties thrown in your honour due to your record profits and bonus payments.

The best way to use this method is to imagine the extremes. If you are someone who finds it easy to make mountains out of molehills, use this skill to create fearful situations. If you're a natural day dreamer, let your mind run wild and picture an abundance of whatever you desire.

Negative-Positive

There will be setbacks – this is guaranteed. It's how you deal with these setbacks that will determine your success. So what are the likely setbacks, and how will you deal with them? How you deal with them is a matter of education – you will simply learn from your mistakes.

The best way to learn is from other people's mistakes but nothing hits home more than your own mistakes. One thing a book cannot give you is experience. While you might follow all the guidance in this book, you will, I hope, still go through the process of making mistakes. The difference between failure and success, however, is that you will turn a mistake into a learning opportunity.

This is the ability to turn a negative situation into a positive one. If you see everything you do as a learning opportunity you can only get wiser as time goes on. This is what experience is all about. There are many mistakes and misfortunes ahead if you do go into business. Below are some that I've made or experienced but have turned around, from a negative situation to a positive one.

Running out of money

Initial reaction (negative)
Any self-respecting businessperson will have faced this. It's known in the game as 'short-term cashflow problems' (i.e. you've run out of cash). When you run out of cash you can become bankrupt.

I ran out of cash as I had over-committed myself. I had assets but you can't pay your bills with assets – you need cash. I was forced to approach a bridging finance company who could raise the cash I needed but they were going to charge me 28% APR. Fortunately I was able to borrow £5,000 from my girlfriend, which just about saved me. It was a stressful time for me as I had to stall certain creditors with lame excuses and I bounced a few cheques and direct debits.

Future action (positive)

Having experienced this you will be determined never to let it happen again. As a result of my experience, I always have a cash float equivalent to six months' mortgage payments for all my properties.

Fortunately I was able to live to tell the tale. I look back now at that situation with a degree of humour. At the time I thought I knew everything about business and I couldn't understand how people could mis-budget, especially a chartered accountant like me. But it was a very humbling experience.

Defaulting by a debtor

Initial reaction (negative)

When I started out I used a letting agent for one of my properties. I went to collect some rent and the owner of this agency told me that his partner had done a runner with the money. I believed him. As it turned out there was no partner. He was a compulsive gambler and had blown the lot on 36 black!

It can be very annoying and frustrating when someone takes your product or service and doesn't pay you. It's easy to think 'is it all worth it?', especially if you've put a lot of hard work into serving or trusting that customer.

Future action (positive)

Question your choice of customer. Did you jump in too quickly because you were desperate for the business? Perhaps in future you will reassess your choice of customer or readjust credit limits for customers so the same doesn't happen again.

It might be time to be a little more sceptical of everyone you do business with. You've got a lot to lose if you don't adopt this attitude and even more to gain.

Being hit by an unforeseen bill

Initial reaction (negative)

I got hit for a £2,500 roof-repair bill early on in my property investment days. Not everything can be budgeted for. Sometimes a bill will knock you for six! This might be a repair, an oversight or an accident.

Future action (positive)

With time you will become less susceptible to unforeseen expenditure. You will budget for the unbudgetable because you have had the experience. You will also question whether the repair is necessary as I do now – do not believe so-called experts. They are only after your money.

Court action

Initial reaction (negative)
I was threatened by a letting agent that they would take me to court unless I paid a £900 fee to come out of my contract. I had little knowledge of the law at that time and if I had had the money I would have paid it – but I didn't have the money.

I spoke to a solicitor friend, read a few books and wrote several letters to defend my situation. Eventually the letting agent gave up.

Future action (positive)
I was forced to educate myself. If it wasn't for this threat I would never have found out how I stood (and now stand) with letting agents. Now I welcome court action in both directions. I recently took one of my tenants to court to evict her and I learnt a great deal from this.

Once you do start enforcing the law you feel more confident in the deals you strike as you know they can be enforced, if need be, in court.

Computer crash

Initial reaction (negative)
I love computers when they work but absolutely detest them when they don't. You only realise how dependent you are on them when they let you down.

This happened recently. I needed to get certain letters out by a deadline and I missed that deadline. I think I looked amateurish to the outside world because my computer crashed and I had no backup. I may have lost some future business due to the computer crashing as my business seems so fragile.

Future action (positive)
Now I have a backup computer. In fact, I have two backup computers! I have learnt that the risk of being unable to print letters, access the web, check your email account or use a spreadsheet can have catastrophic consequences.

The following are some more mistakes and misfortunes that might occur and how to turn them around to your advantage and how to learn from them.

Not enough business to cover your fixed costs

Initial reaction (negative)
Your initial reaction will be 'I'm going to go under!' You may start to look at ways of reducing your overheads but find they're quite inflexible.

Future action (positive)
This forces you to look harder at your business to find out why you're not getting enough sales. Focusing your mind on the most important side of the business (i.e. sales) can only be a good thing in the end.

A few simple changes to your marketing strategy can result in better than expected returns.

Getting too stressed to cope

Initial reaction (negative)
Running a business can be a 24-hour job because the buck stops with you. So if you are facing stressful times these won't stop when it hits 5pm.

It will be difficult for you to relax and to think through the challenges your business is throwing at you.

Your expectations to others are not being met. It's these expectations that are causing you the stress.

Future action (positive)
Setting up a business is front loaded: you do most of the work at the start for a pay-off in the future. Every new business owner goes through this – you are not alone!

Over time you learn to deal with the stress. I used to get very stressed when a tenant did a runner without paying the rent or vandalised my property. Now it takes a lot more to stress me. Recently a tenant burnt down my flat and I didn't bat an eyelid. I have become accustomed to these setbacks as I expect them.

The market changes making your product or service obsolete

Initial reaction (negative)

This can be very worrying and it can happen to anyone. Knowing your market and its fickle tastes is important.

Potentially, all your stock is unsaleable and/or all your skills redundant.

Future action (positive)

The ability to be flexible and to move with the market is the key to success. The lesson is the fact that you can never stand still. You have to know what your customers want at all times.

You also need to be looking out for new opportunities. (See Step 7.)

Being struck by an accident or illness

Initial reaction (negative)

This can happen to anyone. If you're in a business that requires you to be there, to sell the product or provide the service, having an accident or becoming ill is a major problem.

Future action (positive)

If you can adjust your business so it accommodates your setback you've achieved a great deal. Sometimes in life you are tested in situations which you think you cannot cope with. When it actually happens you'll be surprised how well you do cope, thus making you stronger in the future.

Competition

We all have a competitive streak. If you don't, get one! A great motivator is to set yourself against someone else. Schools use this method all the time: we've all sat class exams, and teachers can motivate their pupils by displaying the results in a table with the highest score first. If one of your friends has done better than you you'll be motivated to do better next time. If you're not top but came in the top three you know that, if you work harder, you could come top. Do not be ashamed or guilty of having a competitive streak – it's only natural. My personal opinion is that it's extremely healthy because it forces us to get the best from ourselves.

Pick your competitors wisely, however. It's no good pitching yourself against someone too low or too high. If your competitor is someone you'll beat easily you will become complacent. If he or she is too high you'll become disheartened. Pick a competitor who's slightly better or below you. Typical competitor subjects are described below.

A business competitor you know

This is the most natural competitor to have. If you're not competing against your competitors, this would be worrying. They're in the same line of business, their motivations will be similar and comparing your success relative to them will be easy to measure.

Never be humble about your competitiveness to your competitors, and never feel threatened by the competitiveness of your competitors. This is the real world we live in; you're not in business to be nice – you're in the business of making money and every business should understand this. If they don't, they won't last long.

A business competitor you don't know

Your natural competitor might be too big or too small for you to feel they really are a competitor. It might make more sense, therefore, to pitch yourself against a business that has been in business for the same period of time as you. So if you know of anyone who has just set up in business at the same time as you, use them to chart your success. You might want to compete with a business that is in the same general industry but is not a competitor. For example, if you had a website business you could pitch yourself against another website business even though you have different customers.

A friend or family member

If you've always had a competitive relationship with a certain friend or family member, use this to your advantage. I had a father who always put me down and, in a way, I thank him for that. This pushed me to prove myself at an early age.

If you have someone like this don't let it get to you. Channel this energy in a positive way. Let it push you to do better than even him or her!

Someone you know

You may have come across people you secretly admire. You may not know them well but you know what they do and what they've achieved. They're kind of role models yet you want to do better than them. Remember that imitation is the best form of flattery. So copying, competing and surpassing someone can only be admired – even by the person you did this too.

Goal Setting

Goal setting really does work. It's the one tool that helps people achieve success – including me. I have had many goals in my life and I continue to keep setting them. Some I have achieved, some I have not, some I have revised and some I have discarded. Here are some of the goals I've set including what's happened to them and why.

■ *To obtain my final salary when self-employed within three years.*

Achieved   Not yet achieved

☑   ☐

Discarded   Revised

☐   ☐

I had a realistic goal that was achievable within the time frame I had set. I was earning £1,700 per month when I left work. I wanted to earn £1,000 in year 1 and £1,700 in year 3 through self-employment. Because I had a set figure in mind I was able to plan the expansion of my business so that it could meet these targets. I used to study my Excel spreadsheets and play around with them so I would get my desired result – £1,700 per month! In fact, I surpassed my goal, which you will find happens sometimes, and earned a lot more than my final salary.

■ *To be a millionaire by the age of 30.*

Achieved	Not yet achieved
☑	☐

Discarded	Revised
☐	☐

I wanted to be a millionaire by the time I was 30. This was a goal that wasn't thought through, it was just a goal I had. A millionaire is someone who owns assets worth more than £1 million. As I owned property worth more than £1 million then, technically, I was a millionaire. Having a goal that is positive, even though it's not thought out, is not a bad thing. If it's making you strive towards a theoretical goal it's okay! Everyone likes to have these ill-thought out goals, such as being the richest person in the world or the largest company in the world, so having your own ill-thought targets is fine as long as they're positive.

■ *To have 50 properties by 2002.*

Achieved	Not yet achieved
☑	☐

Discarded	Revised
☐	☐

Again this was another goal I didn't put much thought behind. All I knew was that I wanted to own a significant amount of property, and 50 seemed a decent round number. The key thing is that it was pushing me forward.

■ *To earn £50,000 per month by 2007.*

Achieved	Not yet achieved
☐	☑

Discarded	Revised
☐	☐

I want £50,000 per month as I do not think I could spend more than £50,000 per month. This target ensures I never have to go without when it comes to material goods.

- *To have a Top 40 music hit by June 2005.*
  Achieved   Not yet achieved
  ☐   ☑
  Discarded   Revised
  ☐   ☐

This goal always haunts me. I want it but I just can't seem to knuckle down to achieve it. One of my passions is music but I always seem to get distracted. I often question whether I want it but, ultimately, deep down I know I want to achieve. I think it will be well after 2005 before I achieve it but I have promised myself I will do it.

- *To own a Bentley Coupé before I reach the age of 32.*
  Achieved   Not yet achieved
  ☐   ☐
  Discarded   Revised
  ☐   ☑

I have adjusted this to the age of 35. It's my ultimate car and I will get one but, currently, I simply can't afford it. You are not a failure if you do not achieve your goal in the specified time. It's fine to revise goals. If they're still things you want then obtaining them further down the line is still an achievement.

- *To be a billionaire by the age of 40.*
  Achieved   Not yet achieved
  ☐   ☐
  Discarded   Revised
  ☑   ☐

I wanted to be a millionaire by the age of 30 and I have achieved this. To be a billionaire is really a notional figure that has no real meaning. To be comfortable is an even better goal, which I've equated to £50,000 per month. Hence this is a goal. It's no good busting a gut to achieve a goal when you really have no understanding of why you want it. You need to decide when you are pushing yourself too much. You need to decide whether the goals you are setting are helping you or destroying you.

I hope you've noticed that all the goals had common characteristics:

1. There was a *timescale* – by when?

2. There was a *quantity* – and by how much?

I wasn't saying I wanted more money or more time for myself, I was saying I wanted this amount of time or money by a certain date or age. So when you set your goals, be specific. Put a date and a specified outcome to your goals. Only this way can you monitor if you're on track to success. It's this monitoring that builds confidence, and we all know that having a confident attitude can take you a long way. Two further characteristics that could form part of your goals are as follows:

3. *With whom*. Having a goal to be supplying a certain customer or partnering up with a certain competitor.

4. *Where*. Having a goal to be in a certain geographical location.

When setting your goals, ensure they push you. Do not set easily achievable goals. Use words other people use to help you determine these goals as I did with the words 'millionaire' and 'billionaire'. So it could be the biggest, the richest, the most ethical, the champion or the toughest. Whatever it is, be sure you're heading to be at the top of your game.

Step 7
Staying Out of
the Rat Race

Building and Maintaining Your Position

Staying out of the rat race involves:

- increasing your cash inflow (business) – the business must grow for profits to increase; and

- controlling your cash outflow (personal) – control your personal spending.

OK, so you've got out of the rat race and all you need to do now is to ensure you stay out. This involves not becoming complacent: you must remember one fact of business life – if you stand still you lose. Nothing lasts for ever, especially in business. So if your intention is to create a business that will provide you with a set income level, but you have no growth or efficiency strategy, you will be at the mercy of your competitors. If you decide to spend every penny of your profit on cars or houses you will also be at the mercy of your creditors.

Increasing Your Cash Inflow

There are two ways to increase the cash inflow from your business: duplicating and diversifying or D&D as I prefer to call it. Let's look in more detail at what each one means in more detail.

Duplicating

Duplicate means exactly what it says: if you have an idea that works in one market, simply duplicate it in different markets. Examples of this are all around us (see Table 4).

Business	Original market	Other markets	Description
McDonald's	USA fast-food market	Rest of the world	This is probably the most famous duplication ever. They had one idea (the Big Mac) and took this idea to every country in the world
Tesco	Food retailer in Brighton	In the whole of the UK	On a more local level, Tesco have taken their food retailing idea and brought it to almost every town and city in the UK
Me!	Renting properties in Essex	In the whole of the UK	I found I didn't need to live close to my properties as it wasn't me who had to repair them if anything went wrong. So I just duplicated the rental property idea a hundred times around the UK
Gap	Adult clothing	Children's clothing	They mastered the art of providing trendy clothes at reasonable prices to adults, so they just entered the children's market and repeated the process

Table 4. Businesses that have duplicated.

Can your idea be duplicated or is your business centred on you? Does your service or product require you and you only, or can you delegate? The key to duplication is taking yourself out of the business and getting others to run it for you, i.e. employees.

For duplication to occur you need to do the following.

Ensuring that your profitability is sufficient to take on an employee or employees

If you want to duplicate you need to be sure your profits are sufficient for you to pay someone to do your job. The costs of employing someone are as follows:

- His or her gross pay.

- Employer's national insurance (around 10% of gross pay).

- Employer's liability insurance premiums.

- His or her expenses while doing the job.

- Other benefits you want to give and/or the employee expects.

Remember, your employee must be paid before you, so if you make £2,000 profit per month and you pay your employee £2,000 per month, your own pay is *nil*! As a rule of thumb if you can get an employee to do what you do for one fifth (20%) of your net profit, consider duplication. So if your profit is £100,000 without an employee and you can employ someone for £20,000 a year, duplicate. If your profit is £50,000, forget it; focus on building your profit to £100,000 before duplicating.

Obtaining market research data

First, consider how you want to segment the market. The obvious ways you can carve up a market are as follows:

- **Geographical**.

  Can you sell outside your area or is your product or service restricted to that area only? A shop that sells Liverpool FC merchandise, for example, can only trade in Liverpool itself, whereas a sportswear retailer can trade all over the UK.

- **Age**.

  If your product or service is aimed at a certain age range, consider whether you can sell a similar product or service outside that age range. J.D. Wetherspoon pubs (a successful pub chain) are aimed at drinkers aged over 30. They have now started a wine bar chain (Lloyds) that caters for drinkers aged 18–30. It wouldn't surprise me if they think of something for drinkers aged over 50!

But there are more subtle ways to carve up the market. Consider:

- **Social class.**

  If your product or service is aimed at a certain class of people, find out if you can take that idea to a different class. So if you had a home-delivery food service aimed at the lower working classes (i.e. burgers, chips, etc.) consider adding an upmarket range of dishes (i.e. pasta, paella, etc.) so it appeals to the middle classes.

Once you have identified the market you wish to attack, do some test marketing if possible. Don't just jump in straightaway thinking it will work because it works in the market you are currently in. The type of data you should be able to obtain are:

- people's opinions of your idea in that market;
- competitors and their pricing;
- costs relating to being in that market (i.e. rent, rates, wage costs); and
- Internet and library information on that segment of the market.

You will never have enough data to be completely confident that moving into this new market will be profitable but you will simply have to take the plunge some time. The more data you can gather talking to people, seeking out your competitors and scanning the local press and the Internet, the better will be your chance of avoiding costly mistakes.

Training staff

You will have determined what sort of training you'll need to give your employees. One thing is for sure, however – they will need some kind of training. Do not even consider sending them to any kind of day course, college or residential training centre. You are a small player; this is what larger, more established companies do.

The best person to train them is you. If the reason someone does a good job is due to training *and* experience in the ratio of 20:80 respectively, training is a key part of the process but so is experience – allowing people to make their own mistakes.

Delegate effectively

No one can ever do what you do as well as you and you have to accept this. There will be errors which, sometimes, will be down to you and sometimes down to the people you have delegated to – but it doesn't matter whose fault it is as long as the lessons are learnt.

You must have reasonable expectations of the people you delegate to. Remember, they could be new to the business and be inexperienced. As long as your delegates are:

- loyal and trustworthy;
- hard-working; and
- intelligent enough to do the job

they have the capacity to take your business far.

I employ a rent collector. He is very trustworthy, loyal, hard working and more than able to do the job. He makes mistakes now and again as we all do. But I have a reasonable expectation of him. However, he consistently surpasses my expectations (which is great!) but then, sometimes I forget to be reasonable and expect the earth from him. Try to identify employees who have the attributes mentioned above and try to keep hold of them. If you remain loyal to them they will remain loyal to you.

Adjusting to new skill requirements

The transition from being a one-man band to employing several people is a big one. You have to let go of some skills and replace them with others. The skill you should let go of is as follows:

■ **Day-to-day operational activities**.
Things like admin, individual customer queries, cleaning and anything else that can be done that doesn't require much thought or skill. You need to put a value on an hour's worth of your time. If an hour spent with a prospective customer can generate £500 profit then compare this with the cost of £7 per hour for an employee doing a routine task. It's a simple case of maths!

The skills you should be focusing on are as follows:

■ **Choosing the right employees**.
A business's success is dependent on the people who work for it. If you have the skill of picking the best employees (such as a book-keeper, manager, sales person and technical support person), you have won half the battle. The skill of recognising talent will ensure your success.

■ **Choosing new markets**.
The success of your business requires you to know where there is a good deal and where there isn't. Not only does your own livelihood depend on this but your employees' livelihood, too. Over time your ability to assess risk will be the most important skill you will acquire. It's this ability that separates you from the layperson in your chosen field.

■ **Raising finance**.
The ability to raise finance and to deal with financiers will ensure you'll never go bankrupt.

■ **Being the face of the business**.
To grow, the business requires you to be the best promotional

tool there is. So if you can home in on tricks you know of to gain further business, perfect them! This will involve meeting your customers' and suppliers' decision-makers.

■ **Motivating your workforce.**
You have to be able to manage your staff and this means getting the most from them. Granting responsibility, paying bonuses and treating them with respect are key in this. John Cauldwell (the boss of Phones4U) hit the headlines when he made his top 10 branch managers millionaires by paying them a £1 million bonus as a result of a staggering year's business resulting from their hard work.

Creating and implementing control procedures

If you do manage to duplicate you will need to create and implement the following procedures:

■ Cash outflow control so that you receive all the cash that is generated from your business and to make sure it is not spent on bogus expenses.

■ All the cash resulting from a sale must be recorded and collected so that fraud or theft cannot occur.

■ All laws are being followed concerning your business, including employment law. All this can be found in any good business book.

Diversifying

Diversifying means doing something different from what you are doing. The beauty of diversification is that it lowers your overall exposure to risk because you are not dependent on one single market. So, for example, if you only sold luxury items such as fine wines or cherished registration number plates, you are exposed to the general state of the economy. If we were to go into a recession the demand for such items would diminish, which could put you out of business.

I have the businesses listed in Table 5 that function, as much as they can, independently of each other. All of these businesses were formed by repeating the following steps detailed in this book:

Step 3 – decide what to do and identify the right business for you.

Step 5 – get started and implement the business of your choice.

Step 6 – don't give up – persevere.

So once you've set up a business that's making money, look into doing something that's different. Don't put all your eggs in one basket. I know of many start-up entrepreneurs who have put everything into one idea. Some make it and earn a lot of money but the majority go down – nothing lasts forever. You need to mix and match as much as you can.

Keep abreast of several markets that interest you. Scan the newspapers, talk to people who own their own businesses, talk to customers, suppliers, competitors (if you can) and whoever else is in business. Don't be afraid of asking direct questions about what they're doing. You'll be surprised how upfront some people can

Business	Factors affecting its success	Justification for having such a business
Accountancy practice	You always need an accountant. There are few things that could make the accountant's role redundant	I trained as an accountant so setting up my own seemed the most logical thing to do. It provides a steady income and is the a foundation of all my other businesses
Nightclub and bar	The general state of the economy may affect the amount of disposable income customers have to spend on going out	I spent a lot of my time as a DJ when I was younger so I an understanding of the business. I now understand there's a lot more to the nightclub business than just being a DJ. The returns to be had are enormous if you get it right but this is a high-risk business
Property	People will always need somewhere to live. If interest rates were to rise, however, my profitability would go down	This was my first business and I had already identified the supremacy of property above all other investments. It is relatively low risk and provides me with a solid income that does not depend on to the state of the economy
Cherished number plates	The general state of the economy might affect the amount of disposable income customers have to spend on luxury items	I had an interest in these goods. I started this business because I knew what would sell; it also increases my overall spread of business interests

Business	Factors affecting its success	Justification for having such a business
Book writing	The general state of the economy might affect the amount of disposable income customers have to spend on such discretionary items as books. The Internet poses a threat (albeit a small one) to overall book sales	This is something I love to do but also happen to get paid for. This is passive income: once the book is published you receive regular royalty payments even though you do nothing during this time
Consultancy	Businesses always need consultants. There are, however, a few factors that might make the role of a consultant redundant	I like to meet and chat to new people – so why not get paid for it!
Websites	The website market is a highly competitive one as the barriers to entry are low. This means there are plenty of rivals	Technology excites me. The possibility of becoming a millionaire very quickly, with minimal investment and with a simple but effective idea, keeps me knocking on the World Wide Web door. This is a low-risk business with potentially, huge returns

Table 5. Diversifying your business.

be. I am very upfront about what I do because I hope people will join me. I want to collaborate with others so that we can take ideas further.

Other strategies

Another way to increase your cash inflow (but less exciting) is to control your business expenditure – more precisely, the over-heads of your business. The effect of this can be major or minor depending on how profitable you are. If you're making £200,000 per year and you reduce your overheads by £10,000, this is no big deal. But if you're making a £5,000 loss per year and you reduce your overheads by £10,000 per year, this is a big deal – you are turning a loss into a profit of £5,000.

Fixed overheads to consider when looking to reduce your business expenses are as follows:

- *Rent.*
  Talk to your landlord to see if you can reduce your rent. If you're in a long-term lease this might not be possible, but if your lease is due for renewal and you've been a good tenant, tell the landlord you want a reduction.

- *Wages.*
  Are you getting the best out of your employees? What about subcontracting and only paying for work done rather than having the fixed cost of an employee?

- *Telephone.*
  Consider switching networks to take advantage of deals or other promotions that will keep your phone bill down.

■ *Interest costs.*
If you have borrowings, shop around for a better interest rate. Depending on your borrowings and the payback period, moving lender can have a dramatic effect on your repayments.

■ *Bank charges.*
Many banks offer free business banking for the first year. Even better is banking with a bank that never charges you. Such banks do not offer a business banking service – they simply consider your banking activities as personal banking.

Controlling Your Cash Outflow

If this is this last lesson I teach you, then let it be the one that really lasts. I could go out now to buy myself a brand-new top-of-the-range Bentley coupé *and* an Aston Martin, but I'm not going to. Why? Because the golden rule of business is:

Spend your income not your capital

The basic difference between income and capital is as follows:

Capital – an amount of money that can be invested to return an income.

Income – an amount of money earned as a result of an investment made.

What you deem to be capital is based on your personal circumstances and what you are willing to sacrifice now to invest for the future. For me, a sum greater than £1,000 is a suitable amount to invest. But even £10 is worth investing – it all depends on your circumstances.

When I started my first job I earned £14,000 per year. I spent about £7,000 on my living expenses and invested the other £7,000 (about £600 per month). This £7,000 investment (a total of £35,000) now brings an annual income in excess of £200,000 per year. As a result I was able to buy five properties in three years that gave me an income sufficient for me to leave my job. During the next four years I was able to buy a further 65 properties. I will buy these cars when I earn enough (i.e. when the total HP payment on both these cars is less than 5% of my disposable income).

Also remember that your income will be irregular. It may even be a loss for some months. It is, therefore, no good having liabilities such as a large repair bill for a luxury car when you could be using this money to steer your business through the hard times. As a rule of thumb I spend only 30% of my profit. So if your business generates £3,000 per month, spend only £900 per month. This means £2,100 is saved for the hard times or for future investment. Typical expenditures you should avoid unless you are sure you can meet their payments are:

- mortgage payments for a house beyond your means;
- HP payments for a car that you struggle to even afford a service for; and
- personal loans for such things as holidays, clothes and high-street goods.

In other words, avoid buying liabilities – goods you have to pay for over a long period of time. This will only serve to increase your fixed costs and thus the risk of bankruptcy. Living like a pauper can be a difficult once you've become accustomed to a better lifestyle.

Index

Author's Services

If you need help in leaving the rat race, the author offers a consultancy service to steer you in the right direction. He charges £200 per consultation and can help you with all or some of the steps detailed in this book. If you're interested, contact him at:

Accountants Direct
99 Moreton Road
Ongar
Essex
CM5 0AR

Tel: 0800 652 3979
Fax: 01277 362 563
Email: emergencyaccountants@yahoo.co.uk
Website: www.accdirect.co.uk

You can also subscribe to www.propertyhotspots.net for up-to-the-minute information on property hotspots, property prices, rental yields, property search, estate agents, letting agents, auctions, 100% mortgage providers, buy-to-let mortgage providers, portfolio management and much more.

If you want to know how...

- To buy a home in the sun, and let it out
- To move overseas, and work well with the people who live there
- To get the job you want, in the career you like
- To plan a wedding, and make the Best Man's speech
- To build your own home, or manage a conversion
- To buy and sell houses, and make money from doing so
- To gain new skills and learning, at a later time in life
- To empower yourself, and improve your lifestyle
- To start your own business, and run it profitably
- To prepare for your retirement, and generate a pension
- To improve your English, or write a PhD
- To be a more effective manager, and a good communicator
- To write a book, and get it published

If you want to know how to do all these things and much, much more...

howtobooks

If you want to know how . . . to make money from property

'Many of the world's richest people have made their fortunes from property. Now you can make money from property too – if you are careful. This book will show you how to spot property investment opportunities and how to avoid all the common mistakes. Whether your objective is to add a little to your income in retirement or become a full-time property developer, this book will show you how.'

Adam Walker

How to Make Money from Property
The expert guide to property investment
Adam Walker

'Invest in this book today and make it your first valuable property investment.' – *Amazon Review*

'A guide to many different ways of making money from property, from letting a room to buying land for development.' – *landlordzone.co.uk*

'I was already considering investing in the property market . . . Initially sceptial, I found this book to be my first step on the property investment ladder.' – *Amazon review*

ISBN 1 85703 627 1

How To Books are available through all good bookshops, or you can order direct from us through Grantham Book Services.

Tel: +44 (0) 1476 541080
Fax: +44 (0) 1476 541061
Email: *orders@gbs.tbs-ltd.co.uk*

Or via our website

www.howtobooks.co.uk

To order via any of these methods please quote the title(s) of the book(s) and your credit card number together with its expiry date.

For further information about our books and catalogue, please contact:

How To Books
3 Newtec Place
Magdalen Road
Oxford OX4 1RE

Visit our web site at

www.howtobooks.co.uk

Or you can contact us by email at info@howtobooks.co.uk